DESIGNER KIDS

Consumerism and Competition:
When Is It All Too Much?

DESIGNER KIDS

Consumerism and Competition:
When Is It All Too Much?

David Walsh, Ph.D.

with
Austin Gillespie

DEACONESS PRESS

First Published September, 1990

ISBN: 0-925190-12-8 ✓
Library of Congress Catalog Card Number 90-083227

Printed in the United States of America
95 94 93 92 91   5 4 3 2

Cover Design by Poll Communications Group,
Minneapolis, MN.

Editor's Note: Deaconess Press publishes many books and
pamphlets related to the subjects of chemical dependency and
mental health. These publications do not necessarily reflect the
philosophies of Fairview Deaconess Adolescent Chemical
Dependency Program, nor any 12–Step Program or other
behavioral health program.

Contents

Dedication

To my wife, Monica, and my three children, Dan, Brian, and Erin. These are the four people who gave meaning to this book. In addition, this book is dedicated to my parents, Mae F. Walsh and the late Joseph Walsh, who taught me more than I realize.

Acknowledgments

The ideas expressed in this book took shape over a period of several years and were influenced by many people. Hours of discussion with friends and colleagues were especially important. Special thanks for those hours go to Josie and Bob Donnelly, Karen and Dale Panton, Carol and Ryan Lee Hurd, Meg Leach, Martha Brinson, and Linda Packard. Also, to Cathy Seward and Tom Peichel, who provided support and a quiet place to write.

The support and encouragement for growth is a characteristic of the entire Fairview Organization. Being part of that organization is one of the reasons a project like this could come to fruition. Dottie Jung, Doug Robinson, Mark Enger, Jean Tracy, and Bill Maxwell are some of the Fairview leaders who create that atmosphere.

It has been a pleasure to work with Deaconess Press. Tom Collins was convinced that Deaconess Press should publish *Designer Kids* thirty seconds after hearing the idea. He never wavered in that commitment. Ed Wedman and Bob Italia have been encouraging and very helpful as the manuscript took final form. Their enthusiasm was contagious.

Collaboration with writer Austin Gillespie not only gave expression to the ideas, it refined them as well.

i

Designer Kids began as a seminar I developed in 1987. I originally thought the content would be controversial and expected many challenges from the parents who participated. The reaction has been very positive and encouraging. Their requests for something in writing was what originally prompted me to decide to write this book. The hundreds of parents who have participated over the past three years helped me sculpt the ideas more precisely. Many of the experiences I heard about from parents found their way into this book as examples. My thanks to all of them.

I would like to acknowledge my family in a special way. My three kids, Dan, Brian, and Erin were encouraging, patient, and challenging. Most importantly I would like to thank my wife, Monica. She spent hundreds of hours on this book. The content is as much hers as it is mine. In addition, her editorial suggestions and hours of typing draft after draft were invaluable.

David Walsh, Ph.D.
Minneapolis
September, 1990

Introduction

"Whoever has the most toys wins." "Winning isn't everything, it's the only thing."

These are the warped slogans of our society as we approach the millennium. They highlight our two obsessions: consumerism and competition. We're driving ourselves crazy with these obsessions, and we're teaching our kids to do the same. We're producing a generation of *Designer Kids*.

This book is about the costs and effects of these two overwhelming pressures. It is written by adults who are interested in kids and it is written *for* adults who are interested in kids. It is not written by adults who have all the answers. Indeed it is difficult to identify clear-cut answers to many of the issues raised in this book. Wrestling with the question, however, is important.

This book is about trying to reach a balance instead of wanting everything and wanting it now—even if what we want is a good thing.

The term *Designer Kids* is used in this book to describe the phenomenon of young people who are pushed to be and have the very best of everything. Often their lives are organized by parents and other adults conforming to unrealistic societal expectations and goals. These goals and expectations can pressure a child to accomplish tasks or assume responsibilities which are clearly beyond their emotional maturity. The result is unnecessary stress on a child, with more serious consequences quite possible later on.

From the earliest days of life, parents are making choices and decisions about their child's welfare, education and social experience. In this book, the choices with which I am concerned are those of schools, extra-curricular activities, sports, consumer habits and other matters in the lives of children. I am not referring to the traumatic issues which families may experience, such as the death of a parent or child, divorce, or other major occurrences over which parents have little control.

While it is obvious that the process of growing up has always been stressful in some ways, it is equally obvious that there is more stress now on young people than ever before. We are seeing the symptoms all around us. In the past twenty years there has been a marked increase in chemical abuse among younger and younger children. The suicide rate for children under age eighteen is up dramatically. Eating disorders have become much more common, and instances of depression serious enough to require professional help have appeared with much greater frequency among today's children and young people.

There are undoubtedly many different direct or indirect causes of this increased stress. This book is an attempt to delineate and explore some of the causes about which we can do something. I hope to offer some alternatives to the Designer Kid phenomenon, and remind ourselves that childhood should be a time of discovery, wonder and play, and that too much of any one thing can diminish those important elements.

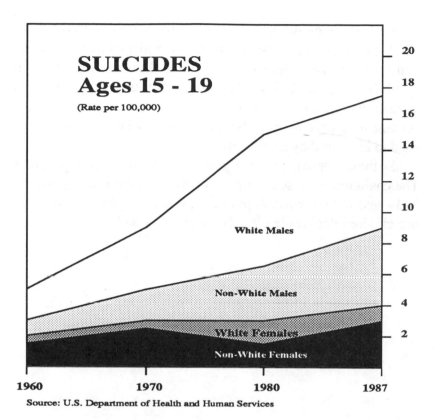

SUICIDES
Ages 15 - 19
(Rate per 100,000)

White Males

Non-White Males

White Females

Non-White Females

20
18
16
14
12
10
8
6
4
2

1960　　1970　　1980　　1987

Source: U.S. Department of Health and Human Services

It would be a too comfortable temptation to pine away for the "good old days." There have been many changes in our society in the past thirty years. Many of those changes are good. It may be fun in a nostalgic sort of way to watch old Ozzie and Harriet re-runs, but we don't live in an Ozzie and Harriet era anymore. Maybe we never did. We live in the 1990s, and our challenge is to figure out how to help ourselves and our children cope with the pressures of the 1990s.

Even if we could go backward in time, it is doubtful that it would be beneficial. Former generations had their own problems. Fathers were much less involved with child rearing and with family life in general. Sex role stereotypes were much more rigid. Women were prevented from equal participation in society just because they were women. No, the "good old days ain't what they used to be; and they never wuz."

So the challenge is not to figure out how to turn back the clock. The challenge is to see our present era for what it is—good and bad—and to take advantage of the good and help ourselves and our children deal more effectively with the bad.

Chapter One

Overview

Why the concern about *Designer Kids?* Haven't there always been children pushed too hard and too fast by anxious parents? Haven't there always been children who had more things than were good for them? What's different now?

Many of us are both victims and perpetrators of an artificially accelerated life-style. Our efforts to acquire a limitless number of things, and our full participation in competition in so many aspects of our lives have led us and our children into a situation which can be unhealthy.

There have been many books written about the significant changes in our society during the past thirty years. The America of the 1990s is very different from the America of a generation ago. We are immersed in a technological and social revolution. Adjusting to rapid and, at times, almost overwhelming changes is bound to bring on stress. Many of these changes, such as the great increase in two-career households and single-parent families, the communications revolution, shifting moral values and drastic changes in the workplace have left people and institutions reeling.

In many cases the changes have raced ahead of our abilities to cope with them. Many of us may be compensating for this feeling of disequilibrium by pursuing material goods, greater job status or indirect gratification through the achievements and accomplishments of our children. It is understandable that we would push our children to compete and acquire—if we are indoctrinated into believing that competition and acquisition are the ways of measuring success in life.

Indoctrinated is not too strong a word. For we are buffeted by messages on a constant basis that scream: "More is better," "Shop till you drop," "More, more, more." Is it any wonder that we may be overdoing it with both ourselves and our children?

The Drive To Be The Best

In considering the stress affecting children, it is important to recognize that the motivation guiding most parents is positive and well-intentioned. It is also entirely understandable. Nearly all parents want what is best for their children, and hope to see them lead successful and satisfying lives. The problem is in defining what is best. Is it in the best interest of a child to be prodded into learning to read before kindergarten —before he or she really has the cognitive abilities to understand the process of reading? Is it in a child's best interest to put in many after school hours over a period of years studying a musical instrument for which he or she possesses neither great aptitude nor interest? And what about the athletically inclined youngsters who make their sport a childhood career, playing or practicing it year-round for so long that they feel burned out by the age of fifteen or sixteen? In a society where the operating slogan seems to be *Go for the Gold*, it isn't surprising that parents and children alike feel pressured to be the best and have the best.

That kind of message is all around us. We see it in advertising slogans everywhere: a bank system's incessant jingle about "Coming in first," a national business newspaper's tag line of "Faster, Tougher, Smarter," and many other similar slogans which beseech us to aggressively get the jump on the competition. We also see that urgency to gain power and top the opposition in the over-zealous approach of some youth athletic coaches, and even in the titles of some recent best-selling books (*Winning Through Intimidation, A Passion for Excellence, Swim With The Sharks Without Being Eaten Alive*). All of these books are marketed and sold with the assurance that their contents will lead the reader to business and monetary success very quickly.

With this message of winning being the only acceptable outcome of any endeavor, it should not surprise us to see an almost desperate determination in our children to compete in the same manner. And from there it is easy to see why we have young athletes going to any extreme to give themselves a competitive advantage—including the use of risky, performance-enhancing drugs such as steroids, or even cheating in the competition itself. So great is the pressure to win that we have lost sight of the value of just making one's best effort. This win-at-all-cost attitude has spread to almost all facets of our culture, and could serve as a partial explanation for the increasing stress on children. So few of their activities seem to exist just for the fun of it. A sense of play seems to have been lost in all the organization and regimentation.

Where a total immersion in studies or arts was once the rare experience of the child of privilege or "born in a trunk" stage kids, now it can be found among children of all backgrounds. Shirley Temple and Jackie Cooper, two of the most successful child stars ever, wrote in their respective autobiographies of a deep unhappiness with their Hollywood childhoods, long-term problems with management of their earnings, and great longing for the kinds of childhoods they imagined other children had. They led much different lives than their publicists led their fans to believe. In Cooper's case, the preparations he was forced to endure for the more heartrending moments of his film roles bordered on child abuse, with directors going so far as to threaten to shoot the boy's dog in order to induce tears for film.

If even the ideal young achievers in American culture have paid a big price for success early on in life, imagine how these stories play out on lesser stages. Once this kind of single-minded pursuit of skills or talent was the rarest of childhood experiences. Now, it is often the kid next door or one of our own who is actively pursuing the dream of sports stardom, entertainment success, or exceptional academic achievement. Ironically, this process seems to be starting at earlier and earlier ages. Why is that? Is it because the media loves to do feature stories on the youth movement in any field? Is it the pressure of parents directing their children to live out their own missed opportunities or fantasies? Or is it pressure our children put on themselves to have and be the best, steered toward even higher goals by advertising and peer pressure?

Society rewards the winners — that's the message we hear and see endlessly. What can parents do in response? Ideally, a balance would be maintained between offering children challenges which are appropriate for their developmental level, and delaying experience and responsibilities for which they may not be ready. That's the ideal. Maintaining the balance is a battle.

The Power of Advertising

The battle does not have clearly defined sides, but there is no doubt that advertising is not on the side of children living balanced lives. The following quote is from a top executive of a large general merchandise chain. "It is our job to make women unhappy with what they have." Although it was listed as a casual tidbit-type of filler in a Sunday newspaper magazine, it speaks volumes about the goals of people with products and services to sell, and the art of advertising that helps them do it.

Anyone who doubts the power of advertising should simply go back and analyze some of the most recent U.S. national elections. Quick-hitting, extremely superficial political advertising has greatly affected the political direction of this country. If advertising can convince people to cast votes based on the kind of media-dominated, insubstantial political campaigns of the recent past, then advertising can be assumed to be very effective in persuading us to buy, believe, and behave in other ways beneficial to the purveyors of that advertising.

By now, advertising has pretty well perfected its technique of persuading us to be "unhappy with what we have," as befits the wishes of the previously quoted businessman. When clever, beautiful-image advertising is focused on young consumers—kids who by their nature and place in the maturing process are just forming self-image and self-esteem—then the effect of manipulative commercials is all the more powerful. Drop the age demographics down a few years and you've got the frantic, rock-music-driven compulsion ads that saturate television programming aimed at children. The overwhelming message of almost all the commercials is: *Get it now!* Of course, the Saturday morning

the worst of all, for it is becoming increasingly
...t to distinguish between many of the programs and commercials for the figures and characters appearing in the programs.

Although regulations exist governing children's programs and the commercials which support them, those regulations can be stretched to accommodate questionable program content and deceiving, distorting ads. It is extremely important for parents to tune in to what their children tune in, so that the ads or programs in question can be evaluated and, if necessary, explained to children for what they are: powerful tools of persuasion used to sell products.

In the past, the need for a parent to explain an outsider's deception might have arisen after a mail order item came back substantially different from what a child expected for the money sent in. Or maybe it was when a parent had to hold back an "I told you so" after a youngster's money disappeared playing what looked like a sure-win game at a fair or carnival. In these times, it's as if we live in an age of the perpetual carny's pitch—and the goal of that pitch is *consume!* "Throw away the old, get the latest version, and here's how to get much more." That is the atmosphere in which we live, and it is an atmosphere which is very conducive to creating Designer Kids—as well as Designer Parents.

The traditional desires of parents for their children (wishing for their success and happiness) and the traditional stressors on young people (anxiety about the future, self-consciousness about self-image and self-esteem) are now the raw nerves for which advertisers aim. Our own doubts help their cause. What we end up with is a variation of keeping up with the Joneses. This time, however, the keeping up involves the achievements of our children, and plenty of stress along the way.

A Matter of Balance

The concept of pursuing high goals and achievements for children should not be condemned. Competition and pressure in the right circumstances can be terrific motivational tools and crucial to a child's development. One can persuasively argue that a certain amount of stress is part of the growth process in people. It absolutely can be a necessary and positive aspect of growing up. (For example, the simple act of leaving home and beginning school, or even pre-school, can have a positive effect on a child. It can encourage independence and cultivate social skills for interacting with other children.)

Nor should we attempt to condemn the pursuit of material possessions. There is nothing wrong with acquiring a reasonable share of comfortable clothes, enjoyable toys, or other items that are part of late 20th Century culture. On the contrary, saving for and obtaining some prized possession can be a source of pride and engender a sense of accomplishment.

Competition and consumerism are not inherently unhealthy factors in a child's development. It is when these two forces get out of balance that the concern grows. It is my conviction that for an increasing number of our children the two C's are out of balance.

There is growing concern that children and adolescents are being asked or being forced to grow up too fast, too soon. In an increasingly competitive world, many parents are inclined, even compelled, to make sure that their children have an edge on the competition—in this case, other children. So it is not surprising that we now have parents reserving places in prestigious pre-schools for children who are still in the womb!

7

Social conditions, material goods, and other elements of daily life have changed drastically since World War II. Those changes have had a great influence on the ways in which children now grow up. We live in an age undeniably dominated by electronic media and timesaving devices, and this has changed the way parents and children live, learn, and understand. The irony is, the more devices we obtain to save time, the less time we seem to have.

Not only have we apparently lost ground in our efforts to gain more free time, we have also blurred the dividing line between adulthood and childhood. What remains is a form of childhood which is low on spontaneous activities and "just for fun" pursuits, and high on anxiety-producing activities.

There is much to benefit from many of these developments and changes of the past thirty years. However, the key to benefiting from the countless choices and opportunities offered to us and our children today is in finding a comfortable balance between planned activities and spontaneous activities, as well as a balance between being busy and finding quiet, reflective times for renewing the spirit. It is finding the balance between the pride of achievement and the drive to win at all cost. It is finding the balance between having nice things and the frantic compulsion to have the latest "in" fashion or gadget immediately.

Our goals as parents should be to encourage our children to learn more and pursue goals, to acquire skills and experiences that will benefit them all their lives while allowing them to grow up in their own ways. We must guard against taking away their natural childhood experiences while possibly replacing them with well-intentioned organized activities. While trying to provide guidance opportunity for growth and new experiences, we also must

supply our own time and enthusiasm to our children. No pro
can replace the valuable personal experiences of spending
and taking active roles in the lives of our children. In subsequent
chapters of this book, I will examine in greater detail the major
themes mentioned in this opening chapter.

Designer Kids

Chapter Two

For Everything There Is A Season

In order to fully understand the problems associated with pushing children too fast or too far, it is important to understand some of the basic principles of developmental psychology. This chapter provides such an overview and creates the context within which the various stressors can better be understood.

As a way of beginning this overview, consider for a moment a young girl about six or seven years old. Let us imagine that this young girl is at the point in her mathematical development where she has mastered the addition of one and two digit numbers. She feels proud of the fact that she can add numbers like 27 and 45 and arrive at the correct answer. She feels particularly competent because this process even involves "carrying," a concept which eluded her understanding just several weeks earlier.

Now imagine someone approaching this girl and presenting her with a square root problem and asking her to figure out the answer. Clearly this would be inappropriate to do and unfair to our developing mathematician. We can hardly imagine an adult doing this because it so clearly violates what we know about how a child's mathematical skills develop.

Our imaginary child in this example is at the stage of her development where she has mastered a skill: addition. Solving a square root problem requires multiplication skills which she does not yet have. Since mathematical skills are sequential, it is not appropriate to skip major steps in the developmental stages.

Although few of us would consider doing this to a child and thus violating obvious developmental sequencing in mathematics there is a danger that we can do similar things in other areas of a child's development.

Just as there are sequential steps in a child's development of mathematical understanding and skills, there are also sequential steps in a child's cognitive and psychosocial development. Ignorance or disregard for these stages can have negative consequences. Unfortunately, there are many forces in our society pressuring us to disregard or violate these stages. The result is that many children who are psychologically at the "simple addition" stage of development are being constantly put in "square root" situations.

Growing Up — It's Just A Stage

The field of study which focuses on stages of development is called, quite appropriately, *developmental psychology.* Throughout this century, developmental psychologists have been learning more and more about how children learn, how they develop language, how they mature emotionally, how they grow socially and about how they progress in conscience formation.

There are a couple of general principles we need to remember about child developmental psychology. First of all, children's developmental stages are sequential. In other words, what happens at one stage affects subsequent stages. To return to our mathematics analogy, skills developed at one stage are the foundation for future understanding and skill building. If I never understand addition and subtraction, this will have an obvious impact on my ability to master multiplication or division. If I never "master" the skill of self-control, this will have an obvious impact on my ability for form and sustain intimate relationships later in my life.

A second general principle of developmental psychology is that there are predictable stages that children (and adults, for that matter) will pass through. For example, children around the age of two will predictably wrestle with issues related to independence and separation. That is why many two-year-olds love the word "no." It's their initial experience of realizing that they are separate from their parents and can state their own preferences and desires.

Although the stages are predictable, we must remember that there is not a rigid timetable that everyone follows in precisely the same way. Nor does everyone deal with the developmental challenge the same. Our understanding of developmental psychology needs to allow for lots of room for individual differences. Temperament, birth order, metabolism, and a host of other factors all contribute to the differences. Any parent with two or more children can probably attest to the fact that individual boys and girls have their own unique personality, style and history of dealing with these predictable issues. It is for that reason that some young teenagers transition into adolescence relatively smoothly while others experience cataclysmic upheaval.

Jean Piaget (1896-1980), a Swiss psychologist, developed a theory of cognitive development in children. Based upon his observations of his own children as well as many others, Piaget identified distinct stages that children pass through as they develop their intellectual abilities. Although modern researchers are refining and in some cases challenging Piaget's cognitive stages, they still provide an excellent framework which helps us understand how children learn.

Erik Erikson (1902-   ) was particularly interested in how children develop psychosocially. Like Piaget's cognitive stages, Erikson's psychosocial stages are the reference points from which many psychologists and educators describe emotional and social growth.

What follows is an overview of a child's development from birth into adolescence incorporating the insights of these two great psychologists.

Figure 1 provides an overview of Piaget's and Erikson's stages and their approximate relationship to chronological age.

Figure 2 and Figure 3 provide a brief and concise description of the stages identified by Piaget and Erikson.

Piaget's Cognitive Stage Theory and Erikson's Psychosocial Stage Theory Related To Approximate Chronological Ages

Age	Cognitive Stage	Psychosocial Stage
17 16 15 14 13 12	Formal Operational	Identity Vs. Confusion
11 10 9 8 7	Concrete Operational	Mastery Vs. Inferiority
6 5 4	Pre–operational	Initiative Vs. Guilt
3 2		Autonomy Vs. Guilt
1 0	Sensori–Motor	Trust Vs. Mistrust

Figure 1

Jean Piaget's Theory of Cognitive Development

Age	Stage

12 -   Formal Operational

Children can reason realistically and deal with abstractions. They can manipulate second order abstractions (eg. algebra) in which letters stand for numbers, which stand for objects. They are able to construct theories thereby helping them form their own identity.

7 - 12   Concrete Operational

Children begin to think logically and organize their knowledge. They can manipulate symbols leading to the ability to read and work with numbers. Rules help them organize their thoughts (eg. grammar) and their world (eg. game rules).

2 - 7   Pre-operational

Children develop language and can use symbols. They engage in elementary reasoning such as the ability to classify and count. They experience the fearful in the world and deal with it through dreams, play, and attachments to symbols (eg. a teddy bear).

0 - 2   Sensori-Motor

Children are involved in active exploration of the world and are obtaining a basic knowledge of objects via their five senses.

Figure 2

Erik Erikson's Theory of Psychosocial Development

Age

0-1 1/2 **Trust Vs. Mistrust.** Through experience children develop a sense that people can either be trusted to help and care for them or else a sense that people cannot be counted on or are even scary or hostile.

1 1/2-3 **Autonomy Vs. Shame.** A child begins to realize he/she is an individual and can do things for him/herself. The child develops a sense of autonomy and capability or develops a sense of self-doubt and shame.

4-7 **Initiative Vs. Guilt.** The child is busy interacting with his/her environment, learning and exploring. The child either feels excited and positive about his/her sense of curiosity or develops a sense of guilt for being inquisitive.

7-12 **Mastery Vs. Inferiority.** The child is involved in school and is expected to perform up to certain standards and expectations. The child develops a sense of him/herself as able to perform adequately or develops a sense of inferiority.

12-18 **Identity Vs. Confusion.** The adolescent confronts the question "Who am I?" by trying out various roles and activities. He/she gradually develops a sense of strengths and weaknesses or becomes mired in a state of confusion.

Figure 3

A Time To Sink Roots . . .
Age 0 - 2

Human beings have the longest period of dependency of any living creature. Infants and small babies are dependent upon adult caregivers for protection, shelter, food, and mobility. In the earliest months, the only things an infant can do to take care of itself is to signal distress through crying. When those signals are met with care and help, the infant learns that people can be counted on and trusted. When those signals are ignored or met with hostility, the infant becomes frightened and begins to develop a belief system that people cannot be trusted or will hurt her. The world is a scary place to such a child.

During the first two years, the child is busy exploring and interacting with her environment will provide optimal conditions for cognitive development.

Anyone who has parented a small baby knows from experience what a demanding task it is. It requires tremendous patience and emotional stamina. Just when the parent is at the point of exhaustion, the baby may signal hunger or pain. Sometimes it requires heroic dedication to comfort a baby with an ear infection through a long sleepless night.

In today's society there is a great deal of pressure on time. With a myriad of demands, responsibilities and activities, it is easy for parents to get stuck on the "fast track" without quite realizing it. Sometimes it seems there is barely time to breathe. Consider, therefore, the dilemma that so many parents find themselves in. On the one hand, time is scarce and the stress is high. On the other hand, there is an infant or young baby who has enormous dependency needs. The young baby needs security, attention, warmth, nurturance, interaction, reassurance, and care.

As we parents make our decisions and arrange our priorities, we need to be aware of the fact that the sense of security and trust that a young child develops does not happen by accident, and can only be nurtured with time and attention. The balancing act of competing priorities is difficult to maintain.

Child psychologists have learned a great deal in recent years about the importance of the formation of the *attachment* relationship. *Attachment* is the term used to describe the close, secure, emotional relationship between parent and baby. If an attachment relationship does not form, then the child will often demonstrate aggressive and under-socialized behavior later on. This attachment takes time, and needs to have a high priority if it is to take place.

There is a Navajo saying that a man cannot be wealthy and a good father at the same time. Although one could legitimately argue the validity of the statement as a generalization, I think it contains significant wisdom about priorities. The sense of the saying is that accumulating wealth and being a good parent are both very demanding tasks. Each requires a great deal of time and energy. But since each demands so much, they are mutually incompatible.

The challenge for us as parents is to maintain a proper balance.

A Time To Sprout Wings . . .
Age 2 - 3

As a child approaches the age of two, she enters the next psychosocial stage and a bit later progresses from the sensori-motor cognitive stage to the pre-operational stage (see Figure 2).

As mentioned earlier in this chapter, the favorite word of a two-year-old often seems to be the word "no." That word is symbolic of a child's changing notion of herself. The younger baby does not distinguish herself from the parent. As the two-year-old develops language, she also begins to realize that she is separate and can have ideas and desires of her own. In some cases, those desires may be contrary to the parents' wishes. The word "no" symbolizes and celebrates that embryonic sense of independence and individuality. At times, the "no" response will be given even when the child complies. It's as if the child is saying, "Even though I'm doing what you asked, I don't really have to."

As the child develops this sense of separateness, she also has the ability to do things for herself. She is able to get around, manipulate objects and perform tasks. As she begins to do things, the question of capability becomes critical. "Am I able to do the things that are expected of me?"

We must remember that this child is still only 1 1/2 to 3 years old. Therefore, the types of expectations for performance are very critical. Parental expectations need to be proportionate with a child's ability. Otherwise the child will begin to have doubts about her ability to perform adequately.

If a parent has appropriate expectations and supports the child's accomplishments, the child develops a sense of autonomy and capability. However, if the parent's expectations exceed the child's abilities, then the child is not able to succeed. The result is a growing sense of self-doubt.

An example which illustrates this is toilet training. Many children begin to master the skill of keeping themselves clean and dry toward the end of this developmental stage. In order to keep herself clean and dry, a child needs to have the ability to connect the internal physical cues with the urge to eliminate. If a child is helped and rewarded for noticing the cues and using the "potty," she can take a sense of pride and accomplishment in mastering this task. Failures or misses are part of the learning process.

Contrast that scenario with one where the parent decides that the child is ready to be "potty trained" and communicates to the child that she should be able to keep herself clean and dry now. For the child who can master the process, everything might be fine. But for the child who does not yet have the ability to recognize the cues, the dilemma is a very real one. "My parent is telling me I should be able to do it. But I cannot figure it out. I can't get it." The result can be a sense of incompetence and self-doubt.

Children master "potty training" at all different ages. There may be averages, but there are wide variations from the averages. The challenge for the parent is to once again strike the balance between encouraging the child to take on new challenges, and not pushing her beyond her abilities to meet the parents' expectations or timetable.

Toilet training is one example out of hundreds of different tasks that the toddler is trying to master. Different children have different timetables and different rates of development. The key is for adult expectations to be realistic so the child masters these tasks with a sense of competence intact.

A Time To Wonder . . .
Age 3 - 7

Anyone who has ever taken a walk around the block with a three-year-old knows that such an excursion can literally take an hour. The child has all sorts of things to investigate during that walk. There's the bark on a tree to feel and pick at. There's an ant hill to observe. There are dandelions to pick. There are sidewalk cracks to excavate with a stick. And all of that is only in the first fifty feet!

Children during this stage have a vivid imagination and a tremendous sense of curiosity. They are learning about the world by exploring and interacting with it. Their sense of curiosity is limitless. If the favorite word of the two-year-old is "no," the favorite word of the four-year-old is "why." "Why is the sky blue? Why don't dogs and cats get along? Why is the sun so bright? Why is thunder so loud?"

This period of curiosity and wonder can also be seen in children's tendency to figure things out and take things apart. They can now use symbols and elementary reasoning. Language is developing by leaps and bounds.

As children interact with a wider world, they also experience the fearful in the world. The fearful shows up in nightmares, worries and in play. This is the age of super-villains and super-heroes. This is the age of great attachments to symbols of security liked stuffed animals and blankets.

Play is critical activity for children during this stage because in play they discover, problem solve, verbalize or dramatize fears, and gain enjoyment. They also learn the art of getting along with others.

All of this takes a great deal of time and patience. Consider the child whose questions are at least acknowledged if not completely answered. Her investigations and discoveries are applauded. Her primitive drawings are exhibited proudly on the refrigerator door. She feels good about her sense of discovery and curiosity.

Consider, on the other hand, the child whose questions are ignored or ridiculed, or the child whose investigations bring reactions of exasperation and frustration from the parent. That child may feel guilty about her sense of curiosity.

The frenetic pace of today's family is not always well-matched to the developmental needs of this child. When I've only got five minutes for that walk around the block, I haven't got time for all those questions. When I'm in a rush, I haven't got time to reassure a five-year-old who is terrified that a wolf is in her closet and is going to attack during the night.

If I want my child to act "grown up," I may not have the tolerance for wild imaginings or terrifying fears.

Once again, what is needed is balance. No parent has limitless patience. No parent can answer all the questions of a five-year-old. That same five-year-old needs to learn that there are limits to the questions and explorations. Not every walk can last an hour. But by the same token, time and patience in large doses are necessary. Freedom to play and to explore are essential.

A Time To Learn . . .
Age 7 - 12

The children during this stage are well into elementary school. They can think logically and organize their knowledge. The ability to read and master mathematics is constantly improving during these years. Socially, they are establishing "chumships" and expanding their social network.

This stage, therefore, involves a great deal of learning in many areas and the development of many skills. Children are quite naturally conscious of how well or how poorly they are doing in this process. Erikson tells us that the biggest question a child has during this stage is: "Can I perform adequately?" In other words, the child is developing a sense of mastery, (i.e. "I can perform adequately") or a sense of inferiority (i.e. "I can't do it right" or "I can't do it well enough").

Children during this stage are very sensitive to the appraisals of their adult mentors whether they be parents, teachers or coaches. If the child is encouraged, supported, assisted, instructed, and affirmed, she will feel capable. If everything is criticized or is never quite good enough, then the child can develop a sense of inferiority.

Children will respond to a feeling of inferiority in different ways. Some children give up and turn away from the activity. Their unconscious logic is: "If I don't try, I can't fail" or "If it doesn't make any difference to me, then I don't care if I fail." An example of this is the student who becomes the class cutup rather than put up with the feelings of inferiority which come from being unable to do school work well enough.

Other children compensate for the feelings of inferiority by overachieving. Their unconscious logic is that "If I do everything perfectly, I'll get recognition and feelings of competence."

The theme of balance is once again critical during this stage. The measure of praise and regard must be balanced with constructive criticism, correction, and discipline which structures and limits behavior but does not denigrate the child is essential.

A Time To Change . . .
Age 13 - 17

Adolescence has been called a "normally abnormal period of life." That tongue-in-cheek description rings true because so much is happening during a relatively short period of time. A child enters adolescence and an adult emerges. That metamorphosis does not occur without its share of ups and downs, trials and tribulations.

The adolescent is undergoing dramatic changes in all areas of her life. She's growing physically, cognitively, socially, and emotionally. She's leaving the land of the little people (childhood) and entering the land of the big people (adulthood). But it's an in-between time. The adolescent is no longer a child but not yet an adult.

The challenges of this period can be summarized in the question: "Who am I?" Teenagers are trying things out, re-evaluating values, challenging parents and distancing themselves from them in an effort to figure out who they are.

The relationship between parents and young children is a very close one. Parents decide where children will live, what school they will go to, what they'll have for dinner, what time they go to bed, etc. So much of a child's life is necessarily controlled by the parent. Then along comes adolescence. The youngster's image of herself begins to change from little person to big person. But who I am as a big person, separate from my parents, has not yet been answered. Therein lies the work of the adolescent. That is to say, they have to answer the question, "Who am I?"

Parenting children is a demanding and challenging task during all stages. Many parents, however, find that it is even more challenging during their children's adolescence. National surveys reveal that parents on the average rate the years they spend parenting teenagers as the most stressful of the parenting careers.

As has been mentioned previously, the theme of balance is critical. There was a popular poster available a number of years ago which read: "There are two lasting bequests we can give our children. One is roots. The other is wings." Striking the balance between roots and wings is, as Adrian Van Kaan said, not a problem to be solved, but more of a mystery to be lived.

Conclusion

This chapter has provided a very brief overview of the main characteristics of the different developmental stages which children pass through. It is not intended to be exhaustive, but rather illustrative and helpful.

This information provides a backdrop or context for the specific pressures or stressors to be examined in succeeding chapters. The word *mature* comes from the Latin *maturus* and means "ripe." The ripening of fruits or vegetables takes time and proper conditions. If certain stressors occur during different stages of the ripening process, then the fruit or vegetable can be damaged or injured.

In order to mature or ripen, children need time and proper conditions as well. There are many forces or pressures. In succeeding chapters, we will explore some of those stressors. As we do so, it will be important to keep in mind the framework of the developmental stages which we have examined.

Perhaps this material could be summarized in these general statements:

1. Children have different needs at different stages. They think and feel differently at different stages.

2. Children don't go through these stages on automatic pilot. Interactions and experiences with adults affect how children progress through those stages.

3. The timetable should not be rushed. Maturing or ripening takes time.

Chapter Three

Adultification of Youth

In the preceding chapter, I discussed the importance of time in the maturing process, and the need for children to address specific issues when they are developmentally ready. Yet one of the greatest pressures on children in our society today is to grow up quickly, a phenomenon I call the *adultification of youth.*

The Quicker the Better

There is a strong bias in American culture in favor of anything fast. Products are constantly promoted on the basis that they are "ready in seconds." *Do it now* is the watchword. We are told that it is foolish to wait for something if we don't need to. If you want to go on a vacation, just go. Don't worry about paying for it till next month's credit card statement arrives.

The bias toward fast and quick has also spread into childhood. Rather than a time of slow ripening, it is increasingly seen as a stage to be gotten through as quickly as possible.

This bias is evident in many ways. Children are pushed to read earlier. Their role models in the media often appear to be grown up well beyond their years. Little Leaguers have full double knit baseball uniforms just like the adults.

In generations past, it was a comic image in a family photo album: a little girl or boy, dressed up in mother's or father's clothes, swimming comically in oversized garments, trying to be a miniature adult. The kids in this type of photo today are just as likely to be dressed in well-tailored versions of adult fashions. Today's Designer Kids are likely to be dressed in $40 designer jeans, $90 shirts, and $150 athletic shoes.

Sexually Precocious

Kids who are encouraged to be like adults are often put in square root emotional situations when they're emotionally only at addition and subtraction. The area of sexuality is an example of this. There is widespread concern about the growing number of teenage pregnancies. Adults are also worried about studies which show that kids are sexually active at younger and younger ages. The statistics should not be surprising, however, since young people are subtly and not so subtly encouraged to be sexually active.

Children are encouraged to dress and behave in sexually provocative ways. It was a few short years ago that Brooke Shields, a young teenager, first appeared in magazine ads with clearly sexual overtones. In her teen years she became almost infamous for print and television ads in which she appeared wearing tight designer jeans, declaring, "Nothing comes between me and my Klein's...*nothing!*"

The message to young girls is clear: it is desirable to be as seductive as possible. Of course, what the jeans maker wanted was more sales, and a deliberately controversial ad campaign was the vehicle chosen for promotion. The advertising industry has never been accused of being troubled by matters of conscience. Since those jeans ads appeared in the mid-1980s, there has been a plethora of similar ad campaigns for various products, featuring ever younger looking seductive models (primarily female) promoting a variety of products ranging from jockey shorts for women, to bubble gum. Yes, bubble gum.

GIRLS SEXUALLY ACTIVE (%)

AGE	1979	1988
15	22%	27%
16	27	34
17	47	52
18	54	70
19	65	78

Source: National Survey of Family Growth —Urban & Suburban Areas

BOYS SEXUALLY ACTIVE (%)

AGE	1979	1988
15	NA	33%
16	NA	50
17	56%	66
18	66	72
19	78	86

Source: Urban Institute

In one television ad broadcast in the spring of 1989, a blonde pony-tailed girl is shown in brightly colored sporty clothes, novelty sunglasses and tennis shoes. It was a confessional-type spot, where the subject is lamenting a chain of events that has made her feel a little down. In a rush of babbled words, punctuated by sharp cracks of chewing gum, she lists the letdowns. Her style is very spontaneous and free-wheeling, and is enhanced by quirky camera work. The camera shots are quickly changing close-ups, profile and wide shots. The girl is dressed junior high style, but her facial expressions suggest a sophisticated sexuality. All this to sell bubble gum, and presented during the Saturday morning cartoon shows—a time when young children make up a clear majority of viewing audience.

This ad is distinctly designed to present a dynamic and exciting figure, one that has associations of peer acceptance and a style that younger children would want to emulate. Again, we have a scenario where the ad does not seem inherently bad, because it is actually lighthearted and airy. It is easy to imagine little children seeing this bubble gum girl as the perfect model for themselves and one whom they would strive to imitate in looks and action. But doing so is completely out of sync with the natural development levels of young viewers of the Saturday cartoon shows.

Unsupervised Kids

Advertising is a major force in the adultification of youth. But it is not the only one. Another major influence on this process is what goes on in the home from a life-style point of view. The life-style matter is one which has undergone sweeping changes in the last two or three decades. The phenomenon of latchkey kids (children left on their own at the start or end of a school day) is but one example of our changing life-styles. Economic demands affect the way our children grow up. In most cases, latchkey situations are necessitated by job schedules. Fortunately, more and more schools are responding to the needs of families for after school programs which offer healthy alternative activities to being locked in a house with only the television for company until mom or dad comes home.

An unsupervised child spending time alone at home will inevitably be confronted with choices and decisions often beyond their years. For safety and security reasons, they may not be free to come and go and play with their friends in an atmosphere made secure and appropriate by adults who are present to set limits and manage the dozens of little crises that come up. The child who has no one to talk with about how the school day went may miss the opportunity to talk through worries, disappointments, and pressures.

Children cannot raise themselves. When they are forced to do so, they inevitably get *adultified* by sheer necessity. Entrusting young children with greater responsibilities has the natural consequence of making them feel more independent and adult-like.

Economic necessity is a reality for many families where a parent cannot be present for significant amounts of time. This discussion is not intended to blame them. It is intended to raise questions about the effects on children when they are unsupervised and how we as a society need to address the issue.

Kids and Television

Another major factor in the adultification phenomenon is television programming. Adult programming has moved into prime time and adult reruns have moved into after school hours. Daytime soap operas are filled with sexually explicit "adult situations." Children are constantly viewing programs which deal with adult themes. People who think children are unaffected by what they see on television are kidding themselves. If we are unaffected by what we see, then why do advertisers spend millions of dollars for the chance to pitch their message? If they weren't convinced they could change our buying behavior, they wouldn't buy time on television. They know we're influenced by what we see on television. That's why they pay so much money for the opportunity to show us their commercials. (For more information on kids and television, see Chapter Nine: *Taming the Tube*.)

No one show will change a child. It's an accumulation of messages constantly repeated over time that gradually influence values, viewpoints, and ways of looking at things.

Percentage of Teens Who Own Their Own Television Sets

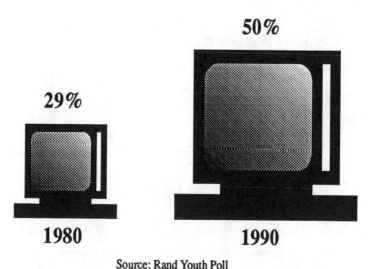

50%

29%

1980   1990

Source: Rand Youth Poll

Kids and Videos

Videos also have a big impact on our kids. The following is an example of one family's experience with restricting just which video cassettes the children would be allowed to view.

Andrew M. is a nine-year-old boy from the Midwest who has the typical variety of interests and influences of most kids his age. And like most kids he is affected by advertisements, television programming, movies, music and clothing styles. He's a good student, readily shows his likes and dislikes on any topic, and loves movies. He cannot understand why there should be any constraints on what he is allowed to see—either at movie theatres or on video cassettes at home.

Number of Hours Watching TV (Per Week)

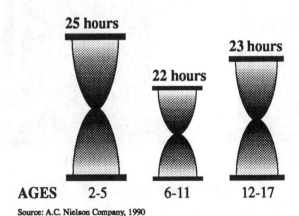

| AGES | 2-5 | 6-11 | 12-17 |

25 hours — Ages 2-5
22 hours — Ages 6-11
23 hours — Ages 12-17

Source: A.C. Nielson Company, 1990

"If you can see any movie, why can't I?" he asks his parents. Some similar-aged cousins and friends at school see most of the new releases, including many of the R-rated ones. Andrew argues that he hears all about the restricted movies anyway, so why can't he see them? To a certain extent, this type of situation is a personal decision between parents, or perhaps between parents and older children. Andrew's parents make a *view* or *don't view* decision movie by movie, or program by program. The R-rating on one movie may be largely for profanity in the script, while another may be for an abundance of graphic violence. They make their choices by previewing films when possible, gathering opinions of other people, or by reading reviews. Their system is flexible, and developed (not surprisingly) by one experience that created the need for it.

Andrew's father recalls the particular incident: "We took out a video called *Revenge of the Nerds* from the public library, thinking that it would be just silly fun for a group of nine- and ten-year-old boys who were over for the afternoon. There was no rating on the video cassette and we didn't think to preview the tape. While watching it with half-attention, it seemed to be just the foolish fun we expected. But then the story took an unexpected turn. One character attempted to get a nemesis' girlfriend so inebriated that she wouldn't realize it was he and not the real boyfriend making love to her. Of course there was no concern for the possible consequences." The tape was stopped to the very noisy protests of the audience. Andrew was furious at the abrupt censorship. In order to explain it to him, his father took him aside. When the boy calmed down after a few minutes, he was given an explanation that included a review of some of the basic facts of life. "I felt that the only way Andrew could understand why his mom and I didn't want him and his friends to see a movie which so badly distorted sexual relations and responsibility was to make sure he understood what love and sex and being responsible was all about. The explanation seemed to satisfy him, and the best thing is that we've talked many times since about personal relations and sexuality. Plus, we really learned to check out movies more thoroughly before we let him see them."

To ignore the influence that videos and movies have on children is to invite images and information into the home which may be either greatly distorted about human relations and sexuality, or certainly far too advanced for many younger children. The same concern should be directed at music videos. While the very visual campaigns of some politicians and public figures protesting the content of pop music and accompanying videos may strike many people as being far too close to blanket censorship, there is no question that there is a need to monitor what our children listen to and view.

Parents Need to be in Charge

Whether the medium is recorded music, video cassettes, cable broadcasting or printed matter, it is important for parents to check out things for themselves, talk things over with the children and, whenever possible, make decisions together about what's suitable. Where younger children are concerned, the discussion will necessarily be less of a give and take effort, and more arbitrary decisions will have to be made. What should be avoided most of all is the absolute banning of any material remotely controversial, with no explanation. This type of action usually results in resentment and an *Us vs. Them* situation between parents and children.

What choices or alternatives do parents and children have to this strong trend toward adultification of youth? To begin with, there really is not a lot of choice about avoiding it. It is now deep in our culture, and becoming more and more entrenched. So the first step in dealing with the adultification process is simply to be able to recognize the ways in which it happens. The awareness of it will enable us as parents to know when our children are being pushed, coaxed, or talked into adopting adult behavior patterns before they are ready.

Secondly, parents need to communicate with their children about this process and about the choices they need to make for themselves. This adultification process can be an opportunity for real learning. Parents can help children make critical evaluations of programs, movies, or music by talking with them about the issues involved.

A parent at one of my Designer Kids seminars offered this example. Her nine-year-old son became enamored of a band which played heavy metal music. Unfortunately, the lyrics of the songs expressed racist sentiments and glorified violence—particularly against women. The nine-year-old boy liked the beat and the sound and had not paid attention to the lyrics. This wise parent knew her son well enough to realize if she simply banned the songs, he would want to hear them all the more. So she listened to the songs with the boy and talked about her disagreement with the values expressed.

She also set some boundaries. They mutually agreed that certain songs were off limits because they were so objectionable. She told him that she didn't care for the band because of the values.

She also told him he could listen to certain songs they played. The talks continued on and off and provided a wonderful opportunity for important value discussions.

The payoff came a couple of months later. The boy was overheard talking with a friend when the subject of the band came up. He informed his friend that this band was "really stupid." "Did you know," he continued, "that they have no respect for women or minorities?" Several days later he told his mother he didn't like the band anymore.

Parents need to determine, situation by situation, just what choice to make regarding fashion, music, entertainment, athletics, and social activities. In the case of younger children, much of this will be determined by specific age. But beyond the strictly chronological consideration, every child is different, and the stages at which he or she is capable of making individual choices will vary greatly. Clearly, these stages of psychosocial development will seldom mesh perfectly with what the child wants to do. The usual experience is that the child or young person strongly insists that he or she is mature enough, adult enough, responsible enough, for anything that life has to offer. The reality, of course, usually falls somewhere short of their tremendous confidence and powers of persuasion.

In this television-dominated era, even very young children may be able to make seemingly sophisticated cases about what they should or should not be allowed to do—and they may be getting their best lines from a favorite television program without grasping the meaning. The important point is that many of the situations which are contributing to the adultification of children are options which parents and children can discuss and analyze, even when the children are very young. Decisions such as buying clothes, choosing a summer camp (or choosing not to attend one), choosing the time and content of television or video viewing are typical subjects which both children and parents can discuss in order to determine how they will fit into our lives. At the same time, the choices we make together can also be made with the thought in mind that the movement to adultify our children too soon can be slowed down by those same choices we make.

Encouraging an athletic son or daughter to diversify interests to other sports outside their specialty can encourage a broadening of interests and possibly reduce the stress which often accompanies a young person's narrow-focus specializing. As noted in the previous example, taking an active role in what music your children listen to and how much time they spend doing it is another area where parental involvement is important and valuable. You do not have to pretend to like modern music, but you ignore it at the risk of not understanding a medium which may greatly influence your children. The goal is not to censor or argue artistic merit.

Once the exclusive realm of young adults, rock and roll music and all the related styles have filtered down to young grade school children. A group can count among their fans many pre-teens. If a particular group also seems to be singing about ethnic groups in an especially negative fashion or about women in a very demeaning manner, and your child listens to it faithfully every day, you should know about it. Better yet, you should be talking about it with your child. When the child affected is very young, rules must be clear about just what can be seen or heard, and why. If this sounds like direct censorship, it is. For whatever reasons, messages in pop music—from blatant racism to advocating violence against women—are depressingly common, even in music played on radio. Unless you have no objection to that type of message being repeatedly sent to your children via some of their favorite rock tunes, you owe it to yourself and them to tune in to what they are listening to.

Conclusion

Here is a review of the major contributing factors of the adultification of youth:

- The practice of targeting consumer goods and marketing at younger and younger people;

- The practice of over specialization at an early age;

- The push at home and school to accelerate the learning process.

There is overwhelming evidence that adultification is a growing trend. Parents and children will have to make concerted efforts to counter the adultification process, or even just reduce its impact and effect on all of us. Kids become adults quickly by any measure. To rush them into it, or allow it to happen too soon is to deprive them of a unique time of their lives, one that can never be replaced. It is up to parents to try and allow children to experience the transition from child to adult in natural time frame, with enough time and opportunity to learn from mistakes, as well as about oneself. Adulthood is a less threatening or confusing time when one has had an opportunity to be a child during childhood. As adults, we owe it to all children.

Designer Kids

Chapter Four

A Passion For Excellence

Certainly, excellence is a positive thing. Excellence has been a goal in a wide range of human endeavors for thousands of years. But can excellence be overdone? A pursuit of *anything* can be overdone—even excellence. Several years ago a book on the best seller list was entitled *In Pursuit of Excellence.* The more recent sequel is entitled *A Passion for Excellence.* From pursuit to passion can mean a transition from a balanced perspective to being out of kilter.

"We're Number One!"

Americans have a fixation on winning. In January, 1990, the Denver Broncos made their fourth trip to the Super Bowl. They had lost in each of their three previous trips. Weeks before the game, columnists and commentators were saying what a shame and disgrace it would be if the Broncos lost again and tied the N.F.L. record for the most Super Bowl losses. As game day approached, there was more talk of the fourth loss than there was about the game itself!

The Broncos did lose the game. Perhaps that is not surprising because the Denver psyche was focused more on not losing than it was on winning. In the days and weeks following the game, there were many columns and articles written about how the entire Denver community sank into depression. There were local Denver media personalities who hoped out loud that the Broncos would never get to the Super Bowl again because the community couldn't take another loss.

But look at reality. How many teams have ever been to the Super Bowl four times? Not many. There were teams sitting at home that day wishing they could be there. The Denver Broncos did very well during an entire season and defeated excellent teams in the play-offs to get to the Super Bowl. Yet the entire community felt deflated, let down, and depressed because they weren't Number One. Number Two is not good enough. Most Bronco fans consider the season a disappointment because they were "only" Number Two.

That same fixation on being Number One permeates much of our society. As a nation we've adopted the Vince Lombardi maxim, "Winning isn't everything, it's the only thing!" What does that message say to our children? In any win-lose competition, there can only be one winner. If winning is the overriding value, then that's fine for the one who wins. But what about those who don't win, but give it their level best? In a class of 28, only one student is at the top of the class ranking. What does being Number One say to the kid who's Number 28? In too many cases it says that he's a failure.

After Designer Kids seminars, I am often approached by parents with horror stories about this fixation on being Number

One. One parent told me about a teacher who always returns test papers in rank order of student's scores. Her daughter often received her paper at the end because her scores were usually low. This parent went on to tell me about the embarrassment and shame her daughter felt as she tearfully told her mother that she was at the bottom of the list again. When the mother talked to the teacher, she was told this procedure was a good motivational tool.

Another parent told me about a high school social studies teacher who announced to his students at the beginning of the term that in his class there were only two grades, A or F. The message was that if your work wasn't excellent, then it was worthless—a failure.

If we remember what was said in Chapter Two about the importance of children feeling competent and successful, we start to get a glimpse of the harmful effects of an overdose of "passion for excellence." Excellence is a relative term for each child. Excellence for a child with limited cognitive abilities may mean that she ranks 28th out of 28 on a math test. If the only measure of excellence is being Number One, then it is very difficult—if not impossible—for that girl to feel proud of her achievement or competence about herself.

Once again, I'm talking about balance. There is absolutely nothing wrong with doing well and achieving. But like anything else, it can get out of balance. That's when the problems arise.

Problems with an over-emphasis on excellence can be seen in many areas of a child's life. Athletics is one of these areas. It has become common for educators to complain about the pressure on students to win in competitive athletics. Recruiting violations and cheating are so common in college athletics that they are hardly newsworthy anymore. Coaches explain that the cheating happens because the only thing that counts is winning. A coach who is a good teacher and wins a reasonable percentage of games will not keep his job at many schools unless his team wins a championship.

Cheating To Win

With winning being the dominant goal, cheating becomes common. High schools report widespread use of steroids in athletics even though the substances are against the rules and pose a serious health threat. The reason they're used is that they will provide a competitive advantage.

A high school hockey coach with a successful program reported how many parents pressured to have him removed because he hadn't taken his team to the state tournament. There are constant problems with coaches recruiting all-star teams among nine- and ten-year-olds in spite of explicit rules prohibiting such recruiting.

Cheating to win becomes common when winning outdistances any other value. Whether it's on Wall Street, on the athletic field, or in the classroom, cheating happens in epidemic proportions when the values get out of proportion. Cheating *is* epidemic, and the values *are* out of proportion.

When winning is the dominant value, other problems happen as well. There was a tragic story reported in a St. Paul, Minnesota suburb several years ago which illustrates the problem. A youth hockey team had traveled out of town for an important game.

Several stars on the team raped a young girl who had accompanied the team as a cheerleader during their overnight stay at a hotel. When she reported the crime, it was *she* who became the object of ridicule and persecution. What she heard was, "How can you press charges? These are the stars of the team! The team cannot win without them! This will hurt their careers!"

The young girl continued to be harassed for blowing the whistle on the stars. Three years later, she committed suicide. Her parents talked about the torment she had endured during those years for "messing up" the team. Those stars had become untouchable because they were "winners"—and winning meant everything.

The Case of the Olympic Burnout

Passion for excellence can also lead to burnout. A recent example involved sixteen-year-old former United States Olympic gymnast, Phoebe Mills, who surprised many people when she announced her retirement from competitive gymnastics and gave the following explanation for it. "I've been away from home and my family for six years, almost. I was really beginning to miss my family."

This 1984 Olympic Bronze Medalist has been suffering from Epstein-Barr virus, a syndrome associated with prolonged fatigue. One has to wonder if the illness was directly caused by a overly rigorous schedule of training and competition. This young gymnast's comments concerning her retirement are important. "It's sort of like a load of pressure has been lifted off my shoulders."

Not long after the gymnast's story was publicized, it was revealed that a large number of former women athletes at the University of Texas had serious eating disorders, especially among members of the highly successful swimming teams of the 1980s. During the eighteen months prior to the publication of this story in the *Austin-American Statesman*, twelve of the University of Texas female athletes were diagnosed with serious eating disorders, most commonly anorexia nervousa (self-imposed starvation) and bulimia (binge eating, then purging food by forced vomiting). Nearly all the cases have been traced to the pressure and training methods of various coaches. A majority of the athletes with the eating disorders were on NCAA championship teams. One team member had gone on to win two gold medals in the 1984 Olympics. Despite her world class success, this star swimmer also fell victim to the pressures of intense competition and a hard-driving coach, and ended up with bulimia and a nine-week hospital stay.

Pre-School Burnouts

A fixation on winning can lead parents to go to great lengths to give their child the competitive advantage. We are not speaking here of simple and basic demands on a child for discipline or responsibilities for school work or fundamental consideration of others. We are speaking about the concerted efforts at giving a child a competitive edge that may be developmentally misguided.

Reading programs aimed at young children are a case in point. There are heavily marketed programs which promise to teach our children to read by the age of four. Those programs make money because parents believe that reading will give them a leg up on the competition. In his book *The Hurried Child*, David Elkind explains that such programs not only do not produce the advantage, but may actually negatively affect a child's reading skills.

There are many preschools which emphasize academic preparation rather than the socialization experience. I recently learned of a preschool where young children were memorizing multiplication tables.

All of these efforts are intended to give a child a jump, an advantage. Research consistently shows, however, that this "advantage" disappears by the middle grades when the older students catch up. In fact, the opposite effect may happen. There is a growing number of educators who worry aloud about eight- and nine-year-olds showing signs of academic burnout.

Eight-Year-Old Professionals

Passion for excellence can also foster what I call "careers that begin at eight." In this pursuit of excellence, more kids get locked into programs that narrow their focus. They are cut off from experiencing a wider range of activities which could help them form a more balanced identity.

The Case of the Retired Gymnast

Recently, I had a conversation with a 23-year-old "retired" gymnast. This young woman explained that she demonstrated gymnastic talents at the age of seven, and over a period of several years became funneled into specialized camps and teams. By the age of ten, gymnastics was a year-round pursuit. All her friends were gymnasts. All her social life revolved around gymnastics. During her adolescence, her identity was formed into that of a gymnast. "I only saw myself as a gymnast," she recalled.

Because of her talent, she won a four-year college scholarship. Throughout her college career, she excelled and participated in national competitions. The crash came at the age of twenty-two when she graduated from college. A gymnast's career peaks very early. After college there was no other path for her to take in gymnastics. So the question arose, "What do I do now? Who *am* I?" She had so defined herself as a gymnast that her identity was completely confused now that she could no longer compete.

Confusion and depression overwhelmed her. She talked to her gymnast friends and discovered that they were all in the same predicament—confused, scared, and depressed. They had no sense of who they were (other than gymnasts) because they had not had the opportunity to develop other parts of their identity. They had missed the developmental stage of adolescence because they were too busy with careers that had started at the age of eight.

More and more youngsters are told that if they really want to be excellent, they have to focus on one particular talent. As a result, they are funneled into groups that practice year-round. Some of the athletes ten or eleven years old are told not to play second or third sports because it will detract from their "careers."

Camp EX-CEL-LENCE

Summer camps are another example of this pressure to specialize, to be more competitive and achieve a higher level of excellence. While there are still many summer camps which offer a variety of activities, there is a dramatically increasing number of specialty camps. The recreational camp experience is frequently spent near a lake or swimming pool. The camps usually have swimming lessons and craft classes. The campers learn new games, memorize camp songs, meet new friends and harass the counselors. Generally, a good time is had by all. The boys and girls return with a little sunburn, maybe a touch of poison ivy, and some happy memories.

Contrast that experience with camps that offer accelerated and intensive schedules as diverse as stock market timing techniques, computer programming, or athletic activities. Campers are guided and molded in a very specific manner for the sole purpose of improving the campers' "talent."

The marketing slogans for some of these camps tell a great deal about their philosophy and objectives. "High-powered hockey training." "Learn, practice, and play golf with the pros." "Instruction (tennis) for fifteen hours a day is available."

These camps are not harmful. But they reflect the current obsession our society has with being Number One and gaining the advantage over the competition. This obsession is very easily transmitted to our children.

Learn by Failing

A philosophy professor in an eastern college used to shock his freshman philosophy students with the following pronouncement on the first day of class: "If something is worth doing, it's worth doing poorly." His point was that part of growing is trying things out—and at times, even failing. Learning from failure can often be more valuable than learning from success. Learning how to cope with failure is an important step in maturing. Our over-emphasis on winning and our passion for excellence can have a number of undesirable results. The child with limited abilities gets the message that he is somehow an inferior or incompetent person. For the child who does win a lot, a great deal of pressure is created to keep coming in first. It can also give that child a distorted view of their own worth with respect to other children.

A Balanced Solution

What is called for once again is balance. Success and excellence are not bad things. But we can motivate our children to do their best without giving them the message that winning is everything. We also need to balance achievement with respect and care for those who haven't been given as much raw talent.

If all hours of practice, study, and honing of skills have not been tempered with the everyday lessons that tell a person that you can't win all the time, then there is a strong possibility that the depths of disappointment can swallow a young person up. No one can be the best in every situation. There can be much pride and satisfaction just participating in an activity. When a passion for excellence means never being satisfied with a best effort, then excellence becomes a tyrant.

Conclusion

It is possible to be competitive without being devastated by not being Number One. Indeed, encouraging that balance between being motivated to compete, and knowing oneself well enough to be satisfied with one's best effort can make a person a more effective competitor. That balance of competitive spirit and high self-regard is a good combination and could make one a calmer, more clear-thinking athlete, scholar, artist, or craftsperson. It certainly makes for a more balanced personality. It also encourages a person to be more accepting and more resilient about life in general.

Chapter Five

Instant Society

Fast, Faster, Fastest

If being Number One is an American obsession, then being Number One very *fast* is an even greater obsession. *Fast* is a great American value. Signs at McDonald's boast, "Your lunch or dinner in sixty seconds or you get a Big Mac Free." A headache remedy that brings relief in thirty seconds is always in danger of losing market share to the remedy that does it in twenty seconds.

Everything we do is in a rush. We have express tellers at the bank, express lanes at the super market, instant potatoes, speedy lubes for our automobiles, books on one-minute management, and one-week diets to lose twenty pounds.

If it takes too long, we as a society are not interested. If fast is good, faster is better. In the past generation, we have constantly found more ways to do things faster. Timesaving devices from microwave ovens to food processors to computers are all designed to gain speed and save time. Theoretically, that saved time should give us more time for relationships, families, and leisure. But in spite of all the timesaving, we have less time than ever before. In the fall of 1989, a national polling company surveyed a cross section of Americans to find out what the biggest concerns were on a day-to-day basis. First on the list was: "Not enough time to do everything." The irony is, after a generation of inventing timesaving gadgets, we feel we have less time than ever before!

The fast pace is evident in many facets of the lives of our children (as discussed in Chapter Two). We rush them to read earlier, learn their numbers earlier, grow up earlier.

Things are presented to children at a very fast pace. The speed with which images flash on the screen during *Sesame Street* is very hard for a teacher to compete with. The popularity of the *Nintendo* game is also related to speed and pace. Things happen very fast in the games, with one or two participants rapidly moving through video mazes, submarine courses, or jungle settings to rescue captured allies, to find treasure or to reclaim lost territory.

To the aural accompaniment of dynamic explosions, forceful fisticuffs, buzzing electronic music and sound effects, a player experiences multiple lifetimes of adventure and mayhem. The games are ingeniously complex with lots of hidden shortcuts. The pace is fast, faster, and fastest. Time penalties create a sense of urgency. Results are quick. A push of the control button annihilates an adversary in a fraction of a second.

Please Me Now!

We like things to happen fast. We don't like to wait. We also like things to be resolved and fixed quickly. We want our efforts rewarded without delay. In other words, we have become a society obsessed with instant gratification. A recent television advertisement captures and plays upon this phenomenon.

The ad presents a beautiful, successful-looking young couple on vacation. They are dining at a luxurious outdoor tropical resort. As they wind up their stay in paradise, the woman looks wistfully at her partner and says in a half-sigh, "It went by too fast, didn't it? I wish it weren't ending." Her male partner responds, "It doesn't have to." The next thing we know, a key phone call is made, all plans and responsibilities are put on hold, and the beautiful couple extends their stay in paradise. All this in less than thirty seconds —thanks to their determination for instant gratification of pleasure, and their credit card.

In fact, their particular credit card company is the one with the slogan, "Membership has its privileges." The same company also proudly touts the fact that there is no cap on the amount of credit available to those with a good record of credit accounts. The whole scenario is presented as a near-fantasy for adult viewers. Most of us *wish* we could do something so capricious, but see it as possible only in our daydreams. The ad's message that a phone call can arrange everything—even a stay in paradise—is the extreme opposite of the kind of work ethic that built this country into a world power, and saw it through two world wars. It flies in the face of the philosophy of working hard to achieve a goal, of being patient, and of the need to save up to earn something worthwhile. With instant gratification messages being promoted on a regular basis, is it any wonder that the American people in general have a declining rate of savings per capita, and that the average American saves a much smaller portion of his or her weekly salary than workers in other comparable industrialized nations?

The direct message from this type of advertising is that we should all be able to have what we want when we want it. Waiting for something is portrayed as a negative infringement on our right to have it now.

Children, by their nature, are impetuous and impatient. They are inclined to want what they want right now. When this natural

Percentage of Personal Income Saved Per Year

1970   4.1%

1980   2.9%

1987   1.7%

Source: Statistical Abstract of United States, 1989

impatience is reinforced in a thousand different ways in our culture, the drive toward instant gratification becomes exaggerated rather than modified.

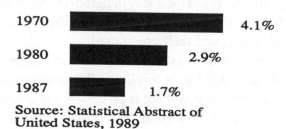

U.S. Credit Card Spending (billions)

1980   John Q. Public   Acct. 0 1234 56 789   Exp. Date 9-9-2000 $205

1985   John Q. Public   Acct. 0 1234 56 789   Exp. Date 9-9-2000 $322

1987   John Q. Public   Acct. 0 1234 56 789   Exp. Date 9-9-2000 $374

Source: Statistical Abstract of United States, 1989

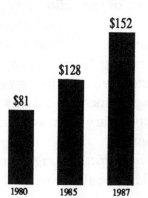

U. S. Credit Card Debt (billions)

$81 — 1980
$128 — 1985
$152 — 1987

Source: Statistical Abstract of United States, 1989

One of the most important skills children need to develop is the ability to *delay* gratification. Many things in life demand perseverance and tolerance for discomfort. Long-term goals can only be attained by patient persistence. Long-term relationships can only be maintained through commitment.

If children are taught that they don't need to wait, then it's very difficult for them to develop life skills which are so important for maturity. Children can be conditioned to expect instant reward either directly or indirectly. The direct message comes from the media which tells kids they should have what they want now. "Don't delay. Act now so we can ship it to you overnight." They are taught instant gratification in the modeling they see in their parents or in other adults.

Thirty Minute Solutions

We are not only taught to get what we want quickly, but we are also taught that difficult problems should be solved quickly. Television shows, for example, portray high human drama and very difficult personal problems. These problems are often resolved in thirty minutes or less. So not only do we have two minute popcorn, but we also have thirty minute resolutions of complicated human dilemmas. Everything is fast. Likewise, problems should be resolved fast.

Elementary school teachers can attest to the impatience of today's children. Often, if a problem cannot be figured out quickly, the youngster wants to give up —or even worse, considers himself to be slow or stupid. After all, competence is equated with lightning-fast problem-solving.

The fast pace of our lives, coupled with the images on television and video games, create a constant state of stimulation and excitement. By comparison, working through complicated math problems or reading a long book may seem boring. Part of life is learning to cope with boredom. But the implicit message of our culture is that boring is bad. Therefore, today's youth is under a great deal of pressure to avoid boredom. What that often means is maintaining a constant state of stimulation. Many children do it with nonstop activities. Many others turn to TV or video games for the stimulation. Anything which cannot measure up in terms of stimulation or excitement is condemned as uninteresting.

Once again, teachers are hard pressed to compete with electronic media. If a school lesson is not entertaining enough, students will entertain themselves or create their own excitement.

No Pain, No Gain

This constant excitement and pressure for instant gratification is often accompanied by an intolerance for pain. Our culture *abhors* pain. We have a remedy for every type of pain imaginable. As a consequence, our children are taught that pain is always bad and needs to be avoided at all costs. This is true of psychological pain as well as physical pain.

I do not want to argue in favor of pain. However, it is part of everyone's life. Therefore, it is essential that we help our children to learn to cope with pain. Coping with pain includes things like perseverance, patience, and the ability to delay reward.

These skills are not learned automatically. They are *taught*. The lessons are not always easy or pleasant. I remember a childhood scene repeated many times over. During the summer, the ice cream truck would make its rounds. As it came down the block, kids scattered in all directions to get money for a treat. Nine times out of ten, my mother would say, "I'm sorry but not today." As I got older, I could argue more forcefully. On many occasions, I accused my mother of being too tight with her money. "Can't you afford a dime?" I pleaded. I can still recall her response. "It's not the money. I just want you to learn that you can't always have what you want when you want it." I didn't understand that lesson at the time, but it's making more sense to me now.

Saying "no" to an insistent child is a lot more difficult than saying "yes." Often, the parents' aversion to the pain of saying "no" leads them to giving in rather than holding the line. Temper tantrums in a discount store or a freeze-out sulk by an adolescent can be painful. It is so much easier to say "yes" (not to mention quieter and peaceful). But what is accomplished? The trouble with always following the path of least resistance is twofold. First of all, the child does not learn the difficult but important lesson about delaying gratification. Secondly, it may create a pattern to which there is no end.

In the case of the "Gimmies" when shopping, the children can be prepared ahead of time as to what they can expect to get (if anything). Deals can be worked out where the latest gizmo will be purchased only as a reward for cooperating or helping, or after a certain amount of allowance or birthday money is saved. If parents can be consistent, their firm response can provide a wonderful opportunity to learn about financial responsibility and the need to delay gratification.

Our everyday actions as adult role models can teach our children a great deal. If our children see us overusing credit cards or shopping constantly without real need, can we realistically expect them to heed our pleas to be patient and do without? We need to remember our children will only hear this message from us. The culture advocates the opposite. Children will hear and see an infinite variety of very persuasive messages to *do it* or *get it now*. The odds are stacked against us. But if parents can be fair, firm, and set good examples, there is a good chance that children will learn this important lesson.

There is a growing concern in our country about our tendency to be a "throw-away society." When something doesn't work, get rid of it. Many household items now are built to be discarded after usage. Disposable lighters, disposable diapers, and disposable food containers are a few examples. The message is clear. It's easier and faster to throw something away than it is to fill it, clean it, or fix it.

This throw-away mentality is very attractive to kids. They tend to be impatient. It is a natural part of their maturing process. Therefore it is not surprising that kids are often ready to discard something when it doesn't work.

The obsession with speed, the avoidance of pain, and the throw-away mentality can all combine to create some very real problems for children as they grow older if those tendencies are not tempered with patience, perseverance, and commitment. Take relationships, for example. Any long-term relationship will have its share of ups and down, joys and pains. If I have learned not to tolerate pain, to discard things if broken, then I will find it hard to honor a commitment through the difficult times as well as the good.

There are few who would deny that one of our nation's most insidious problems is that of drug and alcohol abuse and dependency. Drugs and alcohol are the ultimate quick fix. They relieve pain and provide an instant reward. One of the most addictive properties of crack cocaine is that it produces its euphoric effect in a matter of seconds.

The drug and alcohol problem is multi-faceted. It would be overly simplistic to say that it is a result of our society's attachment to the quick fix for pain. On the other hand, it would be naive to deny any connection. It is not surprising that a society which values very fast results, seeks to avoid pain, and prizes instant gratification has an enormous problem with drugs and alcohol. Those who say that we will never get the problem under control until we address our society's love affair with the quick fix are probably correct.

Conclusion

We return to the theme which has been repeated throughout this book. What is called for is balance. It is a waste of time to grow nostalgic about the slower pace of generations past. We are not all going to get rid of our timesaving devices. We are not going to turn in our automobiles for a horse and buggy. Our culture has changed. We need to learn how to use modern technology, and yet not become enslaved by it.

We have to teach our children how to be efficient with time— and at the same time, patient. We have to teach them that we can't always have what we want exactly when we want it. We have to teach them that part of living involves pain, and that part of growing up is learning how to deal with pain rather than running away from it. We need to remember the words of the poet Eve

Merriam: "There go the grown-ups . . . to the office, to the store. Subway rush, traffic crush; hurry, scurry, worry, flurry. No wonder grown-ups don't grow up anymore. It takes a lot of slow to grow."

Chapter Six

I've Done It All . . . Now What?

Many five-year-olds "can't wait" to go to school for the first time. Seven-year-olds "can't wait" to be eight-year-olds. Fifteen-year-olds "can't wait" to get a driver's license. "Can't wait" is a natural part of childhood, whether it's for a vacation, a trip, a visit from a relative, or a holiday. The natural impatience of youth sometimes makes waiting seem endless and unbearable.

Waiting, however, has two very important benefits for children. First of all, it teaches patience and the ability to delay gratification. Secondly, children have something to look forward to. The first benefit was explored in Chapter Five. The second is the subject of this chapter.

Anticipation Is Half the Fun

Having something to look forward to can provide motivation and excitement in anyone, adult or child. Half the fun of a vacation is in the planning and anticipation. As the count down progresses the energy builds. This is true of short-term goals as well as long-term.

Part of the excitement of childhood is looking forward to the opportunities or privileges coming at a later age. It gives meaning to passages. It can be a thrill to a seven-year-old who gets to stay up fifteen minutes later than when she was six.

All of this obviously presupposes that a child has something to look forward to. If a child is allowed to do everything at a young age, then he has less to look forward to. He has, to a certain extent, already done or experienced it all.

There is a very real danger that this is happening to today's Designer Kids. Kids who do everything at a young age can get easily bored because they have nothing to look forward to. Examples of this can be found in many areas of kids' lives today.

As a result of the adultification pressures discussed in Chapter Three, today's kids do more and more at a young and younger age. More and more adult things are pitched at kids. Advertisers realize that today's kids are not the $2.00-a-week allowance crowd of years ago. It is estimated that the "tweens" (kids between the age of nine and fifteen) spend $45 billion a year.

That burgeoning market is targeted by advertisers of big-ticket adult items like expensive clothes, high-tech sound systems and video equipment. Some school districts are now testing *Channel One* which is a satellite TV station that broadcasts new and youth-oriented entertainment along with hard sell ad campaigns promoting a wide array of products. And there are children's clothing stores specializing in formal wear and high priced designer labels.

There is not just pressure to have adult things at an earlier age. There is also pressure to do adult things at an earlier age. It is not

Billions of Dollars Spent on Advertising (all types)

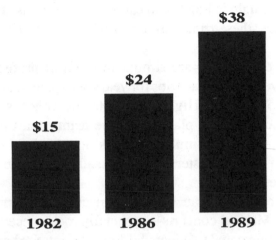

$38

$24

$15

1982   1986   1989

Source: Multi-Media Service

uncommon in many cities for private dance or music schools to rent the area's finest concert halls to hold music and dance recitals for students as young as four years old. Whether they are taking lessons for fun or as the beginning of serious pursuit, children are learning and performing in settings that are as thoroughly professional, high-tech, and state-of-the-art as those used by top professionals.

Should any of these young performers succeed in making a career in the arts, what would they have to look forward to? They have performed on the finest stages already. This kind of acceleration can short circuit the process of gradually building up to special experiences and graduated accomplishments.

Children's athletic programs can offer another example. Young children are often organized into highly structured teams with high quality uniforms. Many take numerous out of town trips staying overnight in hotels and eating in restaurants. For the very elite players, these trips may be to other states or even foreign countries.

These experiences are similar to those of professional athletes. If I've been on road trips for years, what can be special about high school sports? High school athletic coaches have complained that incoming players say the teams don't do anything exciting. A trip fifty miles away is not going to make a big impression on a youngster who has already taken many team trips out of state.

Similar patterns can be found in children's entertainment activities. Musical concerts—especially rock concerts—are targeted to younger and younger children. Parents are barraged with requests from eight- or nine-year-olds to get tickets to the latest concert. These tickets may cost the equivalent of several month's allowance.

The concerts themselves are well-orchestrated events with levels of sensory stimulation that approach or exceed overload. Artists go to greater and greater lengths to outdo one another. After viewing some of these concerts, local events operating on modest budgets pale by comparison.

Social relationship standards are subject to the same pressure. Kids are dating at younger and younger ages. Teachers give examples of boys and girls in elementary school already "going steady."

The problems resulting from kids having and doing things at earlier ages is twofold. First of all, kids have little to look forward to because they've already done so much. This generation of kids is obviously not the first to complain of boredom. "Boring" has been a staple of kids' vocabularies for ages. However the levels of boredom among many of today's youth is a concern. It's hard for them to get excited about everyday life when they've had such a highly stimulating diet.

Money Spent on Food, Entertainment & Clothing by Teens (billions)

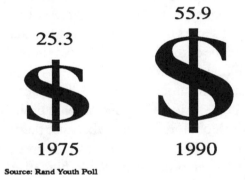

55.9

25.3

1975   1990

Source: Rand Youth Poll

I Need A Bigger Kick

A second problem is perhaps even more serious. As humans, we become accustomed to certain levels of stimulation. Once that happens, we need stronger levels of stimulation to become excited. This is true physiologically and psychologically.

In the chemical dependency field, this phenomenon is called "tolerance." As a person gets accustomed to the effects of alcohol or drugs, then he needs larger and more frequent doses to get the same effect. As tolerance increases, the use escalates until it finally gets out of control.

As kids are exposed to more and more experiences at earlier ages, they develop a tolerance. To feel excitement, they need more and more stimulating experiences. How will kids get pleasure out of a neighborhood or school band concert if they're used to multi-million dollar professional concerts? How will kids be satisfied with holding hands in junior high school if they've been dating for four years?

Many kids who have the freedom to do many things at a younger age become jaded. They are bored with routine day-to-day things. Their senses have been overloaded, and it takes more and more to become stimulated. For them, it becomes a matter of "I've done it all...now what?"

It does not seem unreasonable to hypothesize that this is another factor in the serious drug and alcohol problem among our youth. Drugs or alcohol are attractive because they alter the mood. They give the user a "kick." If a youngster is bored with so much life, it can be very tempting to try something else for that "new kick."

Being aware of this dynamic is very important for adults. It can be so tempting to want our kids to have and do the best. However, we may unwittingly be creating an appetite for stimulation which renders normal life dull and boring. In addition, we rob our children of the excitement of looking forward to special events.

When children are allowed privileges and exposed to different experiences on a graduated basis, they not only have things to look forward to but they also avoid the problem of accelerated tolerance and sensory overload. This principle applies to all areas of a child's life. This does not rule out special treats or special events. But by definition, if something is repeated often enough, it is no longer special.

Conclusion

We can always loosen up restrictions. However, once children accustom themselves to a steady diet of high stimulation, it is very difficult to reverse the trend. We need to be mindful of this as we try to figure out which activities are appropriate for different ages.

The famous singer Peggy Lee popularized a ballad many years ago entitled "Is That All There Is?" Childhood should be a period of discovery and excitement. It would be tragic if those words became the anthem of a generation of kids.

Designer Kids

Chapter Seven

Children As Status Symbols

Because of the intense emotional bond which exists between parents and children, it is very natural and normal for each to have some of their identity at stake in the behavior of the other. For example, children often brag about their parents—at times exaggerating their qualities or achievements. Conversely, children can often be embarrassed or ashamed when a parent makes a mistake or says something foolish. At certain ages, most notably early adolescence, almost everything a parent does can be judged to be embarrassing by the young teen.

A Matter of Pride

Parents likewise take pride in the accomplishments of their children or, conversely, feel embarrassment when their children misbehave. What parent doesn't feel some pride when a son or daughter is chosen for an award? What parent doesn't feel a twinge of embarrassment when a son or daughter throws a full-blown temper tantrum in the middle of the local department store?

Anytime we form a strong emotional attachment to a person or group, we invest some of our identity in that person or group. That is why sports fans feel proud when the local team wins a championship. Emotionally they feel such an achievement reflects on their identity as well. It is for this same reason that companies try to foster employee loyalty. They know that if employees identify with the company, they will feel a sense of pride when the company does well.

These examples illustrate the fact that it is normal for parents to have some of their identity involved in the performance of their children. However, as with anything else, our identification with our children can be overdone. Once again, it's a matter of balance. We need to balance our involvement in our children's performance with a realization that they are separate and independent individuals who must establish their own identity and blaze their own individual trails.

The results of an imbalance in this area can lead to some real problems for kids and parents alike. I'll explore those problems later in this chapter. But first I will discuss some of the influence present in today's society which can lead to an imbalance where parents invest too much of their identity and self-worth in the performance of their kids.

Children As An Investment

First of all, parents today are having fewer children than ever before. This is largely the result of advances in medical technology which enable parents to limit the size of their families. Adults today can decide when and how many children they will have.

Another major development in the past century is that children have changed from being economically productive to economically consumptive. In an agricultural economy, the more children a family had, the more hands there were to help out with the work.

Birth Rate In U.S.
Number of Births Per 1,000 Women

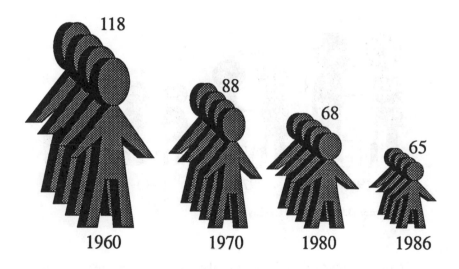

| 118 | 88 | 68 | 65 |
| 1960 | 1970 | 1980 | 1986 |

Source: Statistical Abstract of United States, 1989

In today's urban economy, children do not contribute to a family's income but, rather, consume financial resources. Recent studies now estimate that it costs a family almost $100,000 to raise a child, excluding college costs.

75

The combination of the expense of raising children and the technology which permits family planning choices has resulted in a decrease in the average number of children in a family. In 1960, there were 3.67 children per family. That contrasts with 3.17 children per family in 1988.

Average Family Size in United States

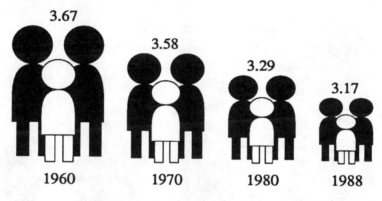

Source: U.S. Bureau of Census

With fewer children in the family, there is a greater amount of concentration of parental attention and emotional energy on the children that are there. More parental hopes, dreams, and aspirations are focused on fewer children. Parental energy in a family of five or six children is inevitably diluted. With only one or two children, there is greater parental concentration.

Do It Right

It is not just the smaller number of children which can contribute to the imbalance. There are other factors as well. Today's parents tend to be better educated and more achievement-oriented themselves. It is very important to do things right. As already discussed, our society has a passion for excellence. This passion can be extended to the role of parent. It is important to do everything just right, including parenting. There are books to raise their I.Q., how to get them into the most prestigious colleges. In other words, our societal drive toward excellence extends to parenting as it does to other areas of performance. Today's well-educated, achievement-oriented parents want to do it right.

compete with other parents

We measure achievement in any area by the results of our efforts. Therefore, it is very understandable that parents look to the performance of their children to measure their effectiveness as parents. In such a system, our children become our report cards. If the children excel and achieve, the parent feels confident that he/she has done a good job. Conversely, if a child is not performing up to parental expectations, the parent may feel a sense of failure.

The competitiveness already discussed in this book extends to the parenting role as well. Parents can unconsciously start competing with one another through their children. Parents can unconsciously start to push their children to perform in a certain way or achieve a certain status so they can look good. This may partly explain the phenomenon of parents competing to enroll their children in the "right" nursery schools or the "right" colleges.

We Are What We Have

Another factor in this equation is the tendency of our culture to measure people's worth by what they have or do. Visible symbols of status signify a person's achievements or worth. The dramatic increase in the number of luxury limousines in the past decade is one example. Society judges people's success by the clothes they wear, the cars they drive, and the neighborhoods they live in. To a certain extent, we are judged by what we have.

This same status symbol tendency can extend to our children as well. If we are not careful, our children can become our trophies which reflect our worth or competence as parents. A child who goes to the best schools, speaks three languages, is an accomplished musician and has great athletic powers can be a status symbol for the adult seeking approval and recognition.

The 1980 movie *Ordinary People* portrayed this dynamic very graphically. In the story, one of two brothers dies tragically in a boating accident. The surviving brother struggles to compete with the memory of the family "hero." At one point, he quits the high school swimming team. His mother hears about this from friends at a social gathering. She is upset and angry and confronts her son in an emotionally powerful scene. What becomes clear during the argument is the main reason for her anger. She is much less concerned with the misery her son is going through than she is with how his behavior made her look.

Certain factors in today's society can put pressure on parents to over-identify with the performance of their children. Parents can over-invest their own identity and self-worth in the behavior and performance of their children. In that event, the balance of normal parental investment becomes distorted. When children become a parental status symbol or measure of self-worth, problems ensue.

A Heavy Load

Parents can unwittingly put too much pressure on their children to overachieve or to engage in activities for which they have neither interest nor aptitude. For instance, imagine the parent constantly pushing a child who is not interested in sports in the direction of competitive athletics. Or imagine the parent who insist that child play the "right" musical instrument or go to the "correct" camp.

Most kids will put a lot of energy into pleasing their parents. Kids who are pushed into activities to meet parents' needs may be burdened with a great sense of responsibility for their parents' happiness. A child who is unable to achieve at a level commensurate with parental expectations can feel incompetent and shameful. In addition, that child may be rejected by the parent because he/she didn't measure up well enough.

One of the most important things a child can develop is a sense of their own worth and independence. Children who have to carry the responsibility for their parents' sense of worth are not free to explore things for themselves, establish their own identity, or make their own mistakes. They do not develop a sense of their own competence.

It is important for parents to focus on the needs and interests of their children rather than their own. The job of parenting involves a level of giving seldom demanded in other areas of life. Parenting involves giving without getting back in return. The true challenge of parenting is captured in the following parable.

The Eagle's Tale

A mother eagle had recently given birth to three baby eaglets. One night, a storm raged through the forest and severely damaged the nest (aerie) where this family of eagles lived. The mother realized the next morning she would need to construct a new, more secure aerie for her offspring. So she went off in search of a suitable location. When she found one, she worked hard constructing the new aerie while alternately feeding and caring for her young.

Finally, after many days, the new aerie was completed. The time had arrived for her to transfer her young to their new home.

Now between the old aerie and the new one, there was a wide and treacherous river with a great number of rocks and white water rapids. As the mother eagle was flying over the raging river with the first eaglet securely grasped in her talons, she looked down and asked the eaglet, "Tell me, how will you treat me when I'm old?"

The eaglet looked up and said, "Have no fear. I will be very grateful. I will make sure your every need is taken care of. I will stay by your side and care for you. You can count on me."

The mother eagle sadly loosened her grip and dropped the eaglet into the raging river.

Returning to the old aerie, the mother eagle gathered up the second eaglet and set out once again for their new home. When they were over the raging river, she looked to the eaglet and said, "Tell me, how will you treat me when I'm old?"

The second eaglet responded, "Have no fear. I will make you very proud of me. I will become the greatest hunter in the forest. I will soar higher than all other eagles. I will do all this for your satisfaction, and you will spend your old age basking in the glow of my accomplishments which will bring honor to you."

The mother sadly released the second eaglet into the raging river.

The mother eagle returned for the last baby eaglet and repeated the trip to the new aerie. When they were over the most treacherous stretch of the raging river, the mother looked down at her baby eaglet and asked, "How will you treat me when I'm old?"

The young eaglet looked into its mother's eyes and said, "Mother, I don't know how I'm going to treat you when you're old. I only know that I will love my children and treat them as well as you've treated me."

The eagle carried the third eaglet to the new aerie, nurtured it, fed it, protected it, and raised it until it was ready to go off on its own.

§

The message of the parable is this: the mother eagle was not parenting her young so that she would be taken care of in her old age. She was not doing it so she could have satisfaction and honor through the deeds of her young. She was interested in rearing independent yet caring individuals who could pass on the same qualities to succeeding generations.

When we can focus on our children's needs and less on our own, when we can give to them without a guarantee of reciprocity, then we can give our children what they need the most. We can give them support, nurturance, love, and guidance so they can become responsible, independent and caring adults. They can then give those same gifts to their children.

Chapter Eight

The Pressure To Consume

The psychology of advertising is based on some rather simple but very powerful principles. Advertisers attempt to create a very positive emotional state in the viewer or listener. They might do this through humor, pleasant imagery, appealing music, or the presence of a popular personality. When that mood or feeling state has been created, the advertiser injects a message about a product. The result is that a particular message or product is linked to a positive feeling state. Therefore, the person exposed to the advertisement is drawn to the product. Much of this linkage happens on an unconscious level.

Power of the Jingle

Although this principle is not terribly complex, it has proved to be extremely effective in shaping the opinions and behavior of millions upon millions of people. With the advances in media technology, the feeling states are more effectively created, and the linkages are stronger than ever. Millions of Americans find themselves being able to repeat advertising slogans or jingles from memory without ever having consciously tried to memorize them. The game *Adverteasing* which was introduced in 1989 is a testimony to the effectiveness of this learning process. The game consists of 2100 slogans, commercials, or jingles which are read aloud. The object of the game is to identify the associated product. Players are amazed at the recall they have about products promoted decades ago.

See if you can complete the following sentence. "Winston tastes good like a . . . " It would not be surprising if the majority of readers could complete the sentence even though it has probably been a matter of decades since hearing it. The jingle "Winston tastes good like a cigarette should" was so well-communicated that millions instinctively remember it years later.

The power of this type of communicating has been focused on the promotion of consumerism in this country for the past seventy years. It was in the 1920s and 1930s that mass production and sophisticated advertising techniques combined to promote the notion of replacing goods out of a desire for something new rather than to replace something worn-out.

Radio Days

This was the era when radio came into its own as a mass medium. It quickly became a vehicle for carrying commercial messages into homes in ways and styles which were completely different. Products literally had their praises sung in the living rooms of target audiences. Newly created radio celebrities talked persuasively about their sponsor's products to listeners as one friend would talk to another. It was one thing to see a celebrity's picture with an endorsed product in a print ad. It was quite another thing to have an admired celebrity talking to you in your own home. Whether it was Bing Crosby for Primo Cigars, Edgar Bergen and Charly McCarthy for Chase and Sanborn Coffee, or a fictional character such as Jack Armstrong, the all-American boy, touting Wheaties, the novelty of radio and the audience loyalty it created was a perfect vehicle for selling things.

The onset of World War II initially slowed down the booming consumerism. Raw materials were needed for the production of war implements and supplies. Conservation became a mark of patriotism. Americans were called upon to make sacrifices of every sort to support the great national endeavor.

Once the war ended, however, the juggernaut of consumerism gathered momentum. First of all, there was pent up demand for consumer products after the period of scarcity during the war. Secondly, skyrocketing birthrates in the post-war baby boom and the rapid growth of suburban communities meant rapidly expanding target markets. Thirdly, there was a new and very potent medium available for the advertising messages: television.

Television

Television proved to be an even more effective medium for communication than radio because it appealed to the visual and auditory simultaneously. Idols could now visit with viewers in their homes as they helped to promote this product or that.

For the past forty years, techniques to promote the purchase of more and more products have been increasingly refined and have become increasingly effective. Obsolescence has been built into more and more products so that replacements will be needed in a short time. Yearly unveilings of new models are now ritualized in a broad array of goods from clothing to automobiles to appliances. The goal is to convince people that the old is bad and to entice people to buy the new.

In order to maintain growth in these industries, people had to purchase more and more. To accomplish this, messages have been communicated to increase consumer motivation to buy. For example, status has been linked to products. The message is, "If you want to be a somebody you have to have . . ." Fashion designers pretentiously affixed their labels to the outside of clothing so other people would know at a glance the status of the person wearing that clothing. It produced a "mine is better than yours" mentality and fueled increased purchasing.

Newer and more subtle avenues for advertising have been discovered. The film industry now enters into product placement contracts. Manufacturers and distributors are offered the opportunity to buy visibility in movies. For a sum of money, they are guaranteed that their products will be used by characters or will be prominently placed on the set. The particular box of cereal on the breakfast table or the specific delivery truck on the street did not get into the movie by accident. They are another avenue that advertisers use to motivate us to buy.

Product identifications with movies and television is not new. The 1950s kids purchased Davy Crockett coon skin caps after seeing their hero on the screen. Mickey Mouse paraphernalia has been sold for decades. It has simply evolved into a more precise science.

Many forms of this commercial cross-pollination have created business opportunities that are difficult to resist. Why not transform *Indiana Jones and the Last Crusade* or *Ghostbusters* into computer games? There are *Nintendo* breakfast cereals and T-shirts bearing the logo of an immense variety of products and places. Saturday morning cartoons are thinly disguised vehicles for product promotion.

Happiness Is . . .

The overall message that consumers hear or see in a thousand variations is that happiness is to be found in things. All of us seek happiness. Therefore, if the messages are effective, we will seek the products linked to happiness. The messages *have* been effective, and millions and millions of consumers have been motivated to buy things as a vehicle to happiness.

The ability to purchase these products means that we have to have money. So it is not surprising that increasing numbers of people are *obsessed* with money. We are being taught that the secret to happiness is wealth. Therefore, the more we can accumulate, the happier we will be.

This is the world we live in. This is the world that today's kids live in. Like everyone else, they are subjected to a nonstop string of messages which exhort them to buy this product or that. They are told in very sophisticated ways that status, happiness, and well-being are found in having enough money to buy things.

Consumer Kids

You are what you have is the message of consumerism. Is it any wonder that kids become fixated on having the right clothes or the right toy? As mentioned in Chapter Seven, kids represent a huge and growing consumer market. Since kids have money, very powerful messages are directed at them. Indications of children's orientation to money and consumerism are plentiful. In 1987, the Internal Revenue Service introduced a children's tax form for kids with investment income exceeding $1,000 a year. Some large city banking companies have opened kids' banks. These banks have kid-sized furniture and teller windows low enough for kids to use. These banks even offer credit cards for juvenile use.

Junior Scholastic offers another sign of the times. In its sixteen page biweekly newspaper distributed to kids between eleven and fourteen years of age, there is an economic section. *Penny Power*, a bimonthly publication exclusively devoted to kids' finances, features such articles as "How to Ask Your Parents for More Money." And as we already know, there are a growing number of summer camps which teach children the intricacies of arbitrage and leveraged buy outs.

The pressure to have the latest can reach tragic proportions. There have been alarming stories of kids robbing other kids for the latest style jacket or radio. Teachers worry out loud about the educational effects of so many students working long hours during the school week in order to earn extra money. Child labor laws are routinely ignored by kids, parents, and employers. Some of these youngsters are working to contribute to the income of a family fighting poverty. However, most are contributing to discretionary income which will go towards the purchase of the next concert ticket or audio cassette. High school administrators can attest to the fact of the need to constantly expand the size of student parking lots since more and more students are driving their own cars.

Soaring Expectations

This rampant obsession with money and consumerism affects the expectations of kids about money. In the spring of 1987, Lynda Richardson and Leah Latimer interviewed a cross section

Percentage of Teens Who Work During School Year

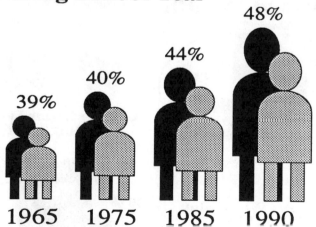

39%
40%
44%
48%

1965   1975   1985   1990

Source: Bureau of Labor Statistics

of graduating high school seniors for a *Washington Post* article. They found startlingly inflated expectations about money across a spectrum of socioeconomic classes. One senior girl confided that she expected to make her first million dollars before she was thirty-five. The authors wrote: "In the schoolyards, hallways and lunchrooms, the talk among seniors this year goes beyond the usual graduation jitters and fears of leaving home for the first time. The talk concerns material success: how best to get it, and what most can deter it."

"I want to be rich—I do!" said one senior. "I know myself," added another. "I'm money hungry." Those sentiments are consistent with a 1986 finding at UCLA's Higher Education Research Institute. In a survey they conducted, 73.2% of incoming college freshmen said it was essential or very important to be

Contrasting Attitudes Toward Wealth

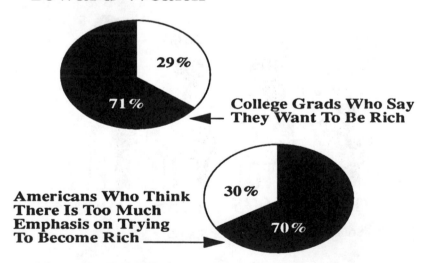

29%

71%

College Grads Who Say
They Want To Be Rich

Americans Who Think
There Is Too Much
Emphasis on Trying
To Become Rich

30%

70%

Source: Gallup Organization, distributed by
Los Angeles Times Syndicate, 1990.

well-off financially. Twenty years earlier, only 43.8% of freshmen had responded that way. "I don't care what it takes," said another senior in the Washington Post article, "I'll do anything to live the life of extravagance."

Economist Dennis Ahlberg of the University of Minnesota has written about the inevitable disillusionment awaiting those with such extravagant financial expectations. He argues that it is mathematically impossible for the economy to support those dreams. What will happen when today's Designer Kids meet that reality?

The impact of this pressure to *buy, buy, buy* can be serious on kids. Preoccupation with money and consumerism can distract them from other more age-appropriate concerns. It is part of the push on kids to grow up too soon. In addition, it creates insatiable appetites for possessions which override other values.

What can be done? You've heard it before: balance. Today's kids cannot be completely protected from the messages of consumerism. But keeping the urges within bounds is essential.

Become Media Literate

Possible things to do

Parents can discuss advertising with kids and help them understand how it works. They can explain how their kids wants are converted to need by sophisticated manipulation. And they can teach their kids over time things which can give us satisfaction. But long-lasting happiness is found in being able to reach out and establish relationships with others.

Ultimately, parents are faced with an important value choice. Are we satisfied with the values communicated to our children in

91

our increasingly consumer-oriented society? If not, then it is up to us to balance them with other values. Perhaps the power of advertising psychology can also be channeled into promoting other messages besides *buy, buy, buy.*

Perhaps *simplify, simplify, simplify.*

Chapter Nine

Taming the Tube

Throughout this book, there have been numerous comments about the influence of various forms of media—primarily television, video, and movies—on the Designer Kids phenomenon. This chapter focuses on that influence. In addition to identifying some of the problems, specific suggestions are made to better manage the media monster.

Two-Edged Sword

Many of today's parents, the baby boomers, were the first generation raised in the presence of a new, powerful, and influential force: television. That medium has proved to be an effective teacher and shaper of behavior. It has opened up new worlds to viewers. It has allowed us to be armchair witnesses to history. Thanks to television, millions witnessed the first steps ever taken on the moon, the horrors of the Viet Nam War, and the exultation of the citizens of Berlin as the wall came down.

Advances in technology allow us to literally see inside a plant's cells, or to observe first-hand the inner working of the human body. The potential of this technology is great. However, as with any powerful tool, the dangers of abuse are as potent as the benefits of its proper use. The same medium that enables us to witness history as it happens or lets us explore the mysteries of nature also expose the average American child to 200,000 acts of violence by the time he/she is eighteen years old.

Visual media—television, videos, and movies—are here to stay. We need to be aware of how they can harm us as well as help. We need to be aware of how they influence our kids. We need to learn how to take charge of these forces in our kids' lives so they will enhance and not harm.

Too Much of a Good Thing...

A 1990 study published by the American Academy of Pediatricians reveals that kids between the ages of six and twelve spend from twenty-two to twenty-seven hours watching television every week. That amount of viewing has been correlated with childhood obesity, sleep disturbances, and aggressive behavior.

Drs. Dorothy and Jerome Singer have spent the past twenty years studying the effects of television on children's development. These two researchers at Yale University have discovered that children who watch the most television tend to be less imaginative, more restless, more aggressive, and have poorer concentration.

Television Violence

Unsupervised television viewing can expose children to a constant diet of violent behavior. Recent additions to programming like *American Gladiators*, *Interceptor*, and *Rollergames* are based on combat between individual contestants or teams. Some fear that Roman gladiator-type entertainment is just around the corner. Others fear it has already arrived!

The rapid growth in popularity of professional wrestling shows is another example. Each month, wrestling promoters concoct more outlandish and more violent scenarios to keep fans and viewers involved. Wrestlers in cages who fight till no one stands are featured. Although the violence in the ring is contrived, the violence among the fans in attendance is not. Security police who patrol the matches can attest to the high incidence of fights and assaults at such events.

The widespread access to cable television and the skyrocketing use of videocassettes have resulted in relaxed standards regarding video violence. A 1990 survey by the National Coalition on Television Violence found that 89% of ten- to thirteen-year-old children had seen at least one episode of *Friday the 13th* or *Nightmare on Elm Street*. Both series bear "R" ratings.

The concern about violence on television and in the movies is that, over time, the viewer becomes desensitized. The excitement generated by one level of violent action gradually subsides with repetition. To stimulate the same amount of excitement, the violence needs to accelerate to another level. As the viewer becomes accustomed to that level, he/she seeks another. This is the reason television and movies have become more and more violent.

Adults and children alike are so accustomed to the violence that we hardly notice it anymore. That's the reason that the previously mentioned statistic of 200,000 acts of television violence in eighteen years comes as such a shock to people.

If television violence didn't affect our behavior, it wouldn't be so bad. The evidence, however, shows that it does. The U.S. Surgeon General's task force on television reported in 1982 that there is overwhelming evidence that T.V. violence increases the tendency toward anger and aggressive behavior.

A 22-year study by Eron and Huesmann found a direct correlation among middle class children between the amount of violent entertainment watched and subsequent aggressive and anti-social behavior. A diet of T.V. violence was the most accurate predictor among a number of factors for juvenile delinquency arrests!

It would be naive to assert that our well-documented problems with violence are simply the result of viewing too much violence on television or in the movies. It would be equally naive to dismiss the influence as inconsequential. The constant unconscious desensitization and the constant role-modeling are bound to have an effect.

Parental Guidance Suggested

As noted in Chapter Three, television and videos are among the most powerful forces in the adultification of youth. Television viewing regularly exposes children to adult situations and is part of the pressure to grow up too soon. Changes in program scheduling, reruns, and access to cable channels result in unsupervised children being able to view adult programs at almost anytime of the day or night.

Television and Consumerism

Businesses with goods and services to sell are the organizations responsible for picking up the tab in the television industry. They pay very large sums of money so they can have the opportunity to convince us to buy their products. Children who watch a great deal of television are spending almost 25% of their time listening to and watching cleverly designed sales pitches. They are being convinced to buy. And, of course, it works. If it didn't, the sponsors wouldn't be spending billions of dollars a year on advertising.

The pressure to consume discussed in Chapter Eight has a very effective medium in the form of television. There are few mechanisms as effective at stimulating the insatiable appetite for things as television.

Television is a two-edged sword. It has the capacity to teach, to inform, and to entertain. It also can be overdone, can desensitize kids to violence, contribute to their adultification, and urge them toward out-of-control consumerism.

No one show will change a child. It's an accumulation of messages constantly repeated over time that gradually influences values, viewpoints, and behavior.

Incentives

We parents need to remember that people who work in television are rewarded for one thing: increased ratings. Whatever increases ratings is what will be telecast. It's simple economics. Increased ratings increase advertising revenues. Television stations are businesses whose goal is to make money for the owners and shareholders. The more people who watch, the more money the television station makes.

Whether or not a show is appropriate for children is irrelevant for most producers. They're paid to produce shows which make money. So the people who bring us television don't have the incentive to develop shows which will help children grow emotionally or cognitively. They're encouraged to develop programs which raise viewership. If violence or explicit sex raise viewership, then that's what will be produced. Many children want to see violence and adult shows. Many children also want to eat a lot of ice cream and no vegetables. We wouldn't dream of letting them exist on an ice cream diet because it is not good for them. They would not develop healthy bodies on an ice cream diet. Yet many of us let our children watch a steady diet of television shows which are not good for their emotional development. Many of our children are being adultified by the television in our homes. The producers don't have an incentive to care. Parents should.

Television is Here to Stay

Television and videos are part of 1990s American culture. And they are here to stay. Forbidding children to watch T.V. is ill-advised for three reasons. First, it's unrealistic. T.V. is too much a part of the fabric of our culture. Second, prohibiting the use of television merely increases its attraction as forbidden fruit. Third, banning television eliminates the very legitimate and worthwhile benefits. There are excellent shows on T.V.

The goal is to help our children learn how to use television appropriately. Some suggestions to achieve that goal are outlined in the following section.

How to Tame the Tube:

1. Avoid using television as a baby-sitter. It might be convenient for busy parents, but it can often begin a pattern of indiscriminant viewing. If children are in a daycare setting, parents should make sure the kids are not plunked in front of a T.V. as a substitute for games or other activities.

2. Limit the use of T.V. There is widespread agreement that while T.V. is not inherently harmful, most children spend too many hours watching it. Its use needs to be limited—and that means turning it off a lot more frequently than we do now.

3. Watch T.V. together. When the television is on, it would be very helpful to watch it—at least some of the time—with the children. This enables parents to be aware of the things kids are experiencing, and the messages they are seeing and hearing. More importantly, it give parents a chance to talk about the programs or advertisements they are viewing. Parents and children can discuss values involved. These can be some very teachable moments.

Parents can also help children understand the techniques of advertising and how we are being manipulated to buy more and more. It also provides parents an opportunity to discuss with children how individuals and families on T.V. are in no way an accurate reflection of the real population. The real world is not nearly so affluent.

4. **Examine how you use television yourself.** The example we set will have a lot of influence on the viewing habits of our kids.

5. **Establish some clear ground rules.** Examples include no T.V. before school, during daytime hours, during meals, or before homework.

6. **Don't turn the set on at random.** Make sure there's a program worth watching before turning on the set.

7. **Do not give the television the most prominent location in the house**. Research shows that people watch less T.V. if it's not the focal point of activity.

8. **Make sure you know what a movie or video is about and how it's rated before you give permission to view it**. This includes what is seen at friends' houses too.

9. **Use the radio, records, or tapes when the television is not on**. Help kids realize that other forms of media are enjoyable too.

10. **Provide alternative activities that are enjoyable.** Simply turning the set off is not nearly as effective as planning some other fun activity with the entire family.

11. **Help the children develop media literacy.** Many schools are requiring media literacy courses. More should. Such courses teach kids which techniques are used to produce certain effects. Children can then be aware that camera angles, lighting, and music are all part of the message. Kids can also be challenged to identify biases or hidden meanings which are being communicated.

Taming the Tube is an important part of parenting in the 1990s. Many of the Designer Kid messages are coming through the television, videos, and movies. We cannot completely control the influence those messages have. Nevertheless, we can manage the effects a lot more. We wouldn't tolerate for a minute having someone standing in our living room telling our kids to do things we know are not good for them. Yet through television, this can happen. We'd better pay attention to what's being said. If we don't agree, we'd better do something about it.

Chapter Ten

What Can We Do?

I began this book saying that the kids of the 1990s are being subjected to very strong pressures toward excessive consumerism and excessive competition. Subsequent chapters identified various specific manifestations of these twin-stressors. The question we are left with is: What can be done to bring more balance into kids' lives?

Throughout this book, various suggestions have been made to provide food for thought and alternatives for parental action. This chapter attempts to identify additional strategies.

I am not presumptuous enough to believe that these are the definitive answers. Rather, they are offered to stimulate thought, discussion, and reaction. Your own list may be somewhat different. You may take issue with some of these suggestions. The important thing is that we begin to wrestle with the issues.

1. Examine Our Own Life-style

Before we can complain about excessive consumerism or competition among our children, we must first look at ourselves. It could very well be that our children are learning these excessive behaviors from us. If we buy on impulse, overextend our credit, shop for recreation, and are always pursuing the latest model car or gadget, then it will be very hard to talk credibly to our children about wanting too much. There is an old saying which may apply here: "I can't hear what you are saying because of the noise of what you are doing."

By the same token, if we become consumed by work, if we are always relentlessly pursuing the next income level and treat leisure as another task to be mastered, then it will be very hard for us to talk to our children about striking a balance in their lives. Many of today's parents may remember the 1970 hit song by Crosby, Stills, Nash and Young entitled "Teach Your Children." It could be that today's Designer Kids have been taught excess by today's Designer Parents.

The theme I have repeated many times throughout this book is that of balance. It seems only fitting that the first place we look for balance is in ourselves. Are we teaching our children balance in the examples we give? Do we exhort our children to limit T.V. watching—and then spend hours in front of the set ourselves? Do we ask them to delay gratification while we rush impatiently to get the latest electronic toy? We may need to re-establish balance in our lives before we can help our kids do the same.

2. Deal with the Present Realistically

I mentioned in the introductory chapter that there may be a temptation to want to turn back the clock to another era. We tend to have euphoric recall about bygone years, forgetting that each generation has its own set of problems and challenges. Although there may be a nostalgic fondness for the 50s and 60s, those decades weren't perfect by any stretch of the imagination.

Trying to return to a bygone era is misguided on two counts. First of all, as just noted, that generation had its set of problems too. Secondly, even if that generation was significantly better, it is impossible to turn back the clock. *Back To The Future* was an enjoyable fantasy, but it was a fantasy nevertheless. This book has focussed on particular stressors or pressures and has identified significant problems. That is not to say, however, that the present age is all negative or is beyond help or hope. On the contrary, this is an exciting age with a growing awareness of global interdependence and an increasing appreciation for the environment. And there are millions of people committed to reducing the injustices of racism and sexism.

Every era has its positives and negatives. The 1990s is no different. We need to deal with the reality we are faced with rather than pine away for a bygone age which will not return. This book has attempted to point out challenges. It is up to us to meet the challenges and chart a slightly different course. This is what parents of every generation must do.

3. Spend Twice As Much Time and Half As Much Money On Our Kids

Designer kids don't need more money. They need more of our time, more of our guidance, more of us. It's too easy for us to soothe our troubled consciences by buying our kids off. All we do is create a greater appetite for things. That appetite is already whetted by the messages which our culture pours out on our kids. Most Designer Kids have enough things.

It is usually easier for parents with disposable income to spend money than it is to re-prioritize our time commitments. It is also easier to spend than it is to wrestle through difficult issues which involve a certain amount of conflict. Taming the spending monster is not easy to do. Retailers and advertisers don't want us to do it. But it is something we must do for the sake of our kids.

4. Say "No"

It is not the responsibility of kids to set boundaries and limits for themselves. That's the job of adults. There are many voices kids hear which tell them to consume, buy more, do it earlier, enjoy it all now. Because of kids' natural impatience, they are more than ready to heed those voices. If anyone is going to set the limits so that balance can be maintained, it has to be the adults in a child's life.

I'm not speaking here of a knee-jerk "no" to everything. Rather, I mean the ability to negotiate meaningfully with our children—but realize that at some point we have a responsibility to draw the line.

It's not an easy thing to do. In short run, "yes" is a much easier word to say. However, in the long run, "no" can be a much more helpful word.

5. Don't Confuse Authoritativeness with Authoritarianism

This suggestion is closely related to the previous one and can cut both ways. Some adults are so nervous about coming off as very authoritarian, they hesitate to set limits or to say "no." Yet some parents say "no" in such a way that there is no room for communication or negotiation. That kind of a firm "no" is called for at times. What is needed more often is dialogue, and give and take. When the harsh "no" becomes the norm, authoritarianism— not authoritativeness—is the result.

Parents have to stand for something and be willing to exercise their authority in setting limits. That's being authoritative, and it provides the security and a sense of direction that children need. They may grumble and groan about the limits. But we need to remember that that's their developmental job. They're suppose to push to the limits. Because they push, that doesn't mean the limits are inappropriate.

6. Communicate

Kids need guidance, nurturing, reassurance, and direction from parents. This only happens if there is effective communication. Kids don't grow up on automatic pilot. They need and deserve the active participation of adults in their lives. Therefore, the time and energy needed to communicate with our children needs to be a priority, not an afterthought.

Communicating is not easy work. It demands skills and patience. It is much easier to buy things for kids to keep them occupied or to let the television—today's "electronic baby-sitter"—do the communicating.

To achieve the balance discussed in this book requires give-and-take, negotiation, the sharing of values, the sharing of feelings, and conflict resolution. These are the ingredients of communication.

7. Communicate with Other Parents

One of the most gratifying results of the Designer Kids seminars has been the parents sharing with one another the concerns and worries they have. Invariably, a parent will voice a concern about excessive competition or consumerism, and other parents will start to nod in agreement or will express surprise to discover that they're not alone with the worry. There can be great relief and support in that type of sharing among adults.

To hear kids talk, every other parent in the universe allows kids to stay up later, watch R-rated movies, buy expensive clothes, and watch more television. The only way we can find out the truth is to talk to other parents. Furthermore, in terms of setting limits, it can be immeasurably helpful for parents to agree on guidelines together and be able to stick to them.

A movement which is picking up momentum around the country is called the *Parent Communication Network.* It is a structure which facilitates this parent-to-parent communication. While many P.C.N.'s are focused on discouraging the illegal use of chemicals, the movement is readily adaptable to address many of the issues raised in this book.

8. Be a Parent, Not a Pal

Our kids have plenty of pals. They only have one or two parents. Parenting is a very unique and important role. Kids need parents who care enough about them to say "no" and to set limits. They need parents who will hang in there with them through good and bad times. They need parents who will give them time to grow, and who will value and cherish them whether they achieve or not. There aren't many pals who can do all that.

9. Don't Overorganize Kids' Activities

Kids need opportunity for spontaneity, play, and unstructured time. They do wonderful things with this time—like develop imagination, role play, daydream, and grow. Some structure and organization is fine. But it can be so overdone. Kids don't need professional entertainers at their birthday parties. They can entertain themselves with games and play. They don't need to have athletic teams with $100 uniforms, four coaches, and four umpires. All they need is a bat, a ball, and a field. Let kids be kids once in a while, even if it is a little chaotic and noisy and "nonproductive."

10. Modify the Competitiveness

Often the kid who could benefit the most from sports is the one most quickly eliminated in a competitive environment. Competition is natural and inevitable. We don't have to do everything we can to intensify and formalize it. Our society needs a lot more cooperation than competitiveness. We need to help our children learn those values through experience and example rather than just through our words.

11. Don't Push Kids Too Early, Academically

Beware of programs that make outlandish claims about child-learning at an accelerated pace or an early stage. What is the advantage of a child learning to read at the age of four if all the other kids catch up a couple of years later, anyway? Kids will learn to read and do multiplication tables in due time. If we push them into it when they should be playing, we run the risk of burning them out, turning them off to the learning process, or obsessive-compulsive personalities. Play is not wasted time. It can be some of the most valuable time a child has.

12. Don't Overburden Children with Freedom to Choose

Children need to be able to make choices which are developmentally appropriate. But we don't want to give them psychosocial calculus problems when they should be in arithmetic. By providing them with structure and direction, they can be free to be kids.

13. Encourage Risk-Taking

Part of childhood is trying things out. When I first try things out, I may not do them proficiently. But "If it's worth doing, it's worth doing poorly." Too early specialization or too great an emphasis on excellence can unintentionally inhibit risk-taking, learning, and maturing.

If the message is perfection, then children may stop developing skills once they find something they're good at. They'll become perfect at this activity, whether it's an academic subject, a sport, or a musical instrument. Since they'll be perfect, they'll be accepted. The tragedy is, they cut themselves off from developing other facets of their personality.

14. Allow Mistakes

Closely related to risk-taking is the tolerance for mistakes—not only tolerance for mistakes, but a *celebration* of them. We certainly learn as much from our failures as we do from our achievements. Not only do we learn lessons, but we develop the capacity to cope with disappointment which is a very important skill.

More importantly, by allowing failure, children will learn that they are acceptable and lovable even when they are imperfect and unsuccessful in a certain endeavor. One of the greatest gifts children can receive is to be accepting and loving of themselves. They can develop into adults who like themselves, are comfortable with themselves, and do not always have to prove themselves by beating someone else or putting someone else down.

It is also important to plan for failure. Kids who are very successful need to learn the valuable lessons which accompany failure and disappointment.

15. Tighten the Purse Strings

Children need to learn the importance and value of money. They also need to learn about the responsibility which comes with having money. If they always get what they want without budgeting, saving, and waiting, they are deprived of those important lessons.

When children express a strong desire for something which costs money, it is important that on at least some of the occasions they have an investment in it. Perhaps they could save up for a percentage of the cost. Or to counteract the "Buy now, pay later" mentality, they could adopt the lay-away approach. That was a purchasing method of a number of years ago whereby an item could be set aside with a down payment, but wouldn't be actually acquired until it was paid for in full.

Whatever the particular approach, we believe some strategy is important to counteract the "Gotta have it now!" frenzy promoted by marketers.

16. Recycle

Recycling not only makes environmental sense, it goes a long way to offset the throwaway mentality which can be harmful to kids. Having kids take responsibility for things can develop an attitude of accountability in many areas of life.

There is one more suggestion. It forms the basis for the final chapter.

Chapter Eleven

A Final Word

Children do not grow automatically into the kind of adults we hope they will become. They are formed and shaped by the messages they receive, and by the environment in which they live. Being a parent entails the responsibility to monitor those messages and shape that environment.

Parenting also requires a great deal of time and energy. Yet many demands compete for our time and energy. So it becomes a matter of setting priorities—no easy task. In spite of the words we hear, parenting is not a highly-valued role in our society. It's given lip service, but little else.

That's true on both a social policy level and a personal level. In terms of social policy, the following statistics call into question our stated commitment to children despite the fact that we are the wealthiest country in the world:

   •Fourteen other countries have higher rates for immunization against polio;

•The infant mortality rate in the U.S. is higher than eighteen other nations;

•Among industrialized countries, only the United States and South Africa do not provide for universal healthcare, childcare, and parental leave for all parents. Legislation to correct that situation was vetoed in July, 1990;

•As a percentage of the Gross National Product (GNP), America invests less than eighteen other countries in healthcare for children;

•Six other countries invest more of their GNP in education than America does.

On a personal level, money, prestige, and power bring recognition, reward, and reinforcement in our society. The role of parent brings none of these. Millions of parents feel caught in the bind between the demands of raising children and the competing demands of work and earning money. Parenting does not bring prestige *or* money. Therefore, it requires great sacrifice and dedication to keep it as a high priority. We need to realize, however, that if we don't dedicate a lot of our time and energy to the role of parenting, our children will be left to grow up on their own.

We are beginning to get some glimpses of what kids raised in the 1980s think about the fast-paced way they were raised. In a 1990 *Time/CNN* poll, 64% of young adults eighteen to twenty-nine years old said they would spend more time with their children than their parents spent with them. After interviewing many of these young adults, writers David Gross and Sophfronia Scott concluded that "they see themselves as having been neglected."

Society gives a double message to parents. We hear, "Children are our future; raising your kids is the most important responsibility." But then the adults who provide childcare are paid below the poverty level, and the full-time parents are asked, "What are you *doing* with your life?" Noted pediatrician-author T. Berry Brazelton states: "I don't think we value children, and we certainly don't value their parents." The fact is, we live in a culture that has very ambivalent attitudes about children and parenting.

Involvement won't happen if it isn't a priority. Our children will be shaped by the messages and influences of society. As we have already discussed, many of those messages promote unhealthy levels of consumerism and competition. Left to those messages, our children will become Designer Kids.

Is that what we want?

And Finally...

The Iroquois have a saying in their treasury of folk wisdom. It reads: "In our every deliberation, we must consider the effect of our decisions on the next seven generations."

That saying can be applied to many of our endeavors. It makes a great deal of sense in regard to the way we treat the earth and the environment. It makes sense when we apply it to political and social policy-making.

It also makes a great deal of sense when we consider the decisions we make as parents. Like generations before us, we are faced with decisions. There are strong forces in our society encouraging our children to consume, accumulate goods at any cost, and win at any price. We have to choose whether to reinforce and confirm those messages, or to temper them with others which call for moderation, balance, simplification, cooperation, and awareness of things and people beyond ourselves.

About The Author

David Walsh is a licensed consulting psychologist and Director of Behavioral Services for Fairview Southdale and Fairview Ridges Hospitals in the Twin Cities metro area. He has worked with individuals and families for over 19 years and has become a regional and national speaker in the area of family and parenting issues. His *Designer Kids* seminars have been enthusiastically received for the past three years and have been the  subject of extensive media coverage, including reports by *National Public Radio*, *The Washington Post*, and by local media in the Twin Cities metro area. His educational achievements include a Ph.D. from the University of Minnesota. Dr. Walsh teaches part-time in the pastoral studies graduate program at the University of St. Thomas. He is married and is the father of three children.

≈

Austin Gillespie is a writer and video producer specializing in family concerns and community affairs. He lives in Minneapolis, Minnesota, with his wife, Janyce Majkozak, and their two children, Andrew and Spencer.

Designer Kids

Other Books and Publications from

DEACONESS PRESS

What's Wrong With Me?—Breaking the Chain of Adolescent Codependency ISBN: 0-925190-14-4, $8.95

Relationships At Risk: Assessing Your Kid's Drug Abuse Potential ISBN: 0-925190-02-0, $6.95

I've Got It Under Control? A Parent's Guide to the First Step ISBN: 0-925190-04-7, $1.75

Little By Little, The Pieces Add Up (Meditations for Teens & Young Adults) ISBN: 0-925190-11-X, $7.95

Life Is Just A Party: Portrait of a Teenage Partier ISBN: 0-925190-05-5, $6.95

Working The Program: The Second and Third Steps for Parents ISBN: 0-925190-13-6, $1.75

To order these books or receive a free catalog,
write to:
Deaconess Press
2312 S. 6th Street
Minneapolis, MN 55454

or call toll-free
1-800-544-8207